Joyce and the Scene of Modernity

David Spurr

University Press of Florida

Gainesville · Tallahassee · Tampa · Boca Raton

Pensacola · Orlando · Miami · Jacksonville · Ft. Myers

Copyright 2002 by David Spurr
Printed in the United States of America on acid-free, totally chlorine-free paper
All rights reserved

07 06 05 04 03 02   6 5 4 3 2 1

Library of Congress Cataloging-in-Publication Data
Spurr, David, 1949–
Joyce and the scene of modernity / David Spurr.
p. cm.—(The Florida James Joyce series)
Includes bibliographical references and index.
ISBN 0-8130-2550-8 (c.: alk. paper)
1. Joyce, James, 1882–1941—Criticism and interpretation. 2. Popular culture—Ireland.
I. Title. II. Series.
PR6019.O9 Z8116 2002
823'.912—dc21   2002019470

The University Press of Florida is the scholarly publishing agency for the State University
System of Florida, comprising Florida A&M University, Florida Atlantic University, Florida
Gulf Coast University, Florida International University, Florida State University, University
of Central Florida, University of Florida, University of North Florida, University of South
Florida, and University of West Florida.

University Press of Florida
15 Northwest 15th Street
Gainesville, FL 32611-2079
http://www.upf.com

For my mother and father

Contents

Illustrations

Foreword

David Spurr's study covers some already cultivated ground but offers new and original contexts for Joyce studies as well as for other modernist writers along the way. The study also offers a number of significant fresh interpretations of Joyce's works. Essentially a miscellany of nine essays, Spurr's work serves as departure for "a reflection on the nature of literary modernism and its relation to modernity" in general.

The introduction does a good job of tying the entire collection into a continuum of contemporary critical theory, using the ideas of most of the major current social/theoretical suspects: the post-Marxists, the psychoanalytic and neocolonial theorists, the language analysts, and the revisionist intellectual theoreticians. Joyce's work is seen in four principal contexts: (1) the political, including Irish nationalism; (2) the social/cultural, in exploring the effects of urbanization and mass communication; (3) the intellectual, as a part of the developing thought of major intellectual historians of the period; and (4) the literary, in comparison with other major modernist writers, notably Eliot and Proust.

Zack Bowen
Series Editor

Acknowledgments

Parts of this book have appeared elsewhere: chapter 1, "Colonial Spaces in Joyce's Dublin," appeared in *James Joyce Quarterly* 37.1/2 (2002); chapter 3, "Anthropologies of Modernism: Joyce, Eliot, Lévy-Bruhl," appeared in *PMLA* 109.2 (March 1994); chapter 6, "Fatal Signatures: Forgery and Colonization in *Finnegans Wake*," appeared in *European Joyce Studies* 8 (1998); and chapter 7, "Writing in the *Wake* of Empire," appeared in *MLN* 111.5 (1996). Permission to reprint these essays is gratefully acknowledged. The photographic illustrations to chapter 1, "Colonial Spaces in Joyce's Dublin," are reprinted courtesy of the National Library of Ireland.

I wish to thank friends and colleagues on both sides of the Atlantic for their helpful comments on various aspects of the work represented in this volume. These include Fritz Senn, Astradur Eysteinsson, Ellen Carol Jones, Zack Bowen, and Laurie Spurr. I am also grateful to Pascal Griener for inviting me to present a version of chapter 2, "The Comedy of Intolerance in Proust and Joyce," at the University of Nantes as part of France's celebration of the four hundredth anniversary of the Edict of Nantes.

A Note on the Translations

Unless otherwise noted, translations of French quotations are my own.

Abbreviations

CW   James Joyce, *The Critical Writings,* edited by Ellsworth Mason and Richard Ellmann (Ithaca, N.Y.: Cornell University Press, 1989).

D   James Joyce, *Dubliners* (New York: Penguin, 1992).

FW   James Joyce, *Finnegans Wake* (New York: Penguin, 1959). Citations refer to page and line numbers.

U   James Joyce, *Ulysses: The Corrected Text,* edited by Hans Walter Gabler (New York: Vintage, 1986). Citations refer to chapter and line numbers.

P   James Joyce, *A Portrait of the Artist as a Young Man,* edited by Seamus Deane (New York: Penguin, 1992).

Introduction

Altereffects

The essays in this volume bring together two distinct critical movements in the recent study of literary modernism: one studies the relations between works of modernism and contemporaneous historical events; the other reads the texts of modernism, and Joyce in particular, in the light of the questions posed by literary theory. The aim of the first of these movements is to place modernism "in context," that is, to examine literary works in terms of the fairly immediate historical conditions of the epoch in which they have been produced. These conditions include not only events of global significance such as the Great War but also those aspects of ideology and consciousness that belong to everyday life and that together may be said to constitute a "subjective" modernity developing in relation to objective conditions represented in the space of the city; in the institutions of nationalism, imperialism, and colonization; as well as in political or social movements contesting conventional notions of race, gender, and sexuality. "Contextual studies" differ from traditional historical studies of literature both in the density of the material they bring to bear on their subject—in this resembling contemporary movements in historiography and anthropology—and in their analysis of the literary work in terms of a wider culture marked by relations of power and economic interest.

Whether one holds, with Astradur Eysteinsson, that modernism is essentially subversive of those relations, or with Fredric Jameson, that it perpetuates them through a purely aesthetic vision of their effects, modernism is nonetheless seen primarily as engaged in an evolving universe of social forms. There is emphasis here on the literal meaning of the literary "work," on literature as a product of labor, which in turn works within or against a specific set of material conditions. Cheryl Herr, for example, reads Joyce's work as a "literature of exposure" that lays bare the ideology of certain institutions of Irish popular culture at the beginning of the century: the press, the stage, and the pulpit (Herr 6). More recently, Lawrence Rainey studies the modernist literary movement as a series of publishing ventures calculated to gain ascendancy in the cultural marketplace. The work of Herr and Rainey represents the best of a historicist approach to Joyce, the limits of which become evident in less accomplished hands: a tendency to be bound by "facts" and the objective relations between them, to read literature as little more than documentation of contemporary events and ideas. Such studies foreclose on discussion of the human necessity of literature at any given historical moment and of the ways in which literary works may address the more fundamental questions of modern existence. They are limited in their capacity to take account of both the specificity of literary language and the role of literary works as the symbolic expression of human desire.

Such questions are precisely the preoccupation of the other critical movement with which I am concerned, a style of inquiry more consciously theoretical and more philosophically oriented than the study of historical context as it is normally conceived. Here the emphasis is on "text" rather than work, that is, on the nature of literary language itself as a function of what it means to be human. Thirty-five years ago, Paul de Man described the then-new French literary theory as being engaged in an "ontology of the poetic," referring to writers who, drawn toward the question of being, "try and always fail again to define human existence by means of poetic language" (1989, 156). This is the critical project that asks how literature is possible, and that finds fertile ground in literary modernism and its aftereffects. In a variation on T. S. Eliot's image of art as constituting an ideal order of existing monuments (1975, 38), Maurice Blanchot writes of modern writers who, when entering the space of literature, find it to be a temple filled with murmurs that alter in advance what one is able to say. This temple must be both destroyed and recreated in the act of writing, so that "to write is ultimately . . . to refuse to 'write'" (1995, 147). The characteristically modern situation of the near-impossibility of writing is not so much a question of refusing traditional literary conventions as it is a radical questioning of the literary act itself.

The project defined by Blanchot and Roland Barthes, carried forth by de Man, and given new life by Jacques Lacan and Jacques Derrida, is still very much alive. One of my aims, both here and in the essays that follow, is to demonstrate that this theoretical project, far from being abstracted from questions of historical context, is in fact motivated by the specifically modern situation that Blanchot describes, and that it has gone a fair distance in helping to explain the precise nature of the relation between the texts of literary modernism and the objective conditions of modernity.

Lacan's psychoanalytic theories have had important consequences for the interpretation of Joyce's work by such critics as Jean-Michel Rabaté, Garry Leonard, and Christine van Boheemen-Saaf. Lacan's idea of Joyce as "symptom" refers, at least in the first instance, to that element of Joyce's work which sacralizes the human body and in which language itself functions as fantasy, that is, as the symbolic manifestation or symptom of bodily desire. But whereas in other writers the forms of linguistic expression are made more or less intelligible by their relation to a more general symbolic order, Joyce has recourse to an "epistemic babble" (*bafouillage épistémique*) that deliberately resists this order in the name of a being-in-speech (*le parlêtre*) that Lacan proposes to substitute for the Freudian unconscious. Hence the unique and exceptional nature of Joyce as a writer, whom Lacan qualifies as both symptomatic and saintly (*symptôme* and *saint-homme*). And hence the celebrated unintelligibility of Joyce's language in its purest form (in *Finnegans Wake*), as unintelligible as bodily *jouissance* itself: "jouissance opaque d'exclure le sens" (the opaque enjoyment of excluding sense) (Lacan 1979, 17). Ellie Ragland-Sullivan draws an analogy between the bodily, embodied quality of Joyce's language and Lacan's designation of the Real: "The inert energetics of a *jouissance*, both unsymbolized and empty yet totally dense and full, that Lacan attributes to the Real, constitutes the painful, silent symptom behind Joyce's language" (173). Van Boheemen-Saaf carries this point even further, making the "event" of Joyce's writing into a crucial point in the development of Lacan's thinking. She points out that Lacan's reading of Joyce in the 1970s forced him to alter his view that the "real" lay somewhere safely outside the realms of the symbolic and the imaginary. This view was undermined for Lacan when he recognized in Joyce's text "an instance of the binding of the real onto the symbolic and into history, as well as a dramatization of the usually repressed consciousness of the material determination of human subjectivity" (van Boheemen-Saaf 1999, 8).

This is where Lacan's work takes on a specifically historical dimension. The result of Joyce's binding of the real onto the symbolic is a "mimesis of loss," a new kind of writing that dramatizes the failure of symbolization, the void of unrepresentability that in Joyce's case, van Boheemen-Saaf argues, is related to the historical trauma of Irish colonization (1999, 11). What is important to note for my purposes is the way that readings of

Joyce inspired by Lacan have succeeded in retrieving Joyce's unintelligibility from the status of mere linguistic anarchy. Instead, the denseness and opacity of Joyce's text, notably in *Finnegans Wake* but also present in the earlier works, can be seen as embodying those very qualities of the real that underlie the symbolic and that constitute the interstices of symbolic texture. Understood in this manner, Joyce's text is more intimately related to its historical context than is suggested by traditional notions of historical representation. This must be taken into account in reading what would appear to be Lacan's militantly ahistorical reading of Joyce: "Joyce denies that anything happens in what history, as understood by historians, supposedly takes as its content. He is right, history being nothing more than a flight in which only exoduses (*exodes*) are recounted" (1979, 15). Lacan seems to say here not just that history is the story of exile and exodus, but also that that which is taken to be the study of history is itself a flight from the real circumstances of human existence. "Historical" readings of Joyce would then be a pretext for avoiding the most pressing questions posed by his extraordinary language, a language engendered precisely by the crisis of representing historical reality.

If Lacan's figure of the symptom is essentially synecdochic—seeing Joyce as the manifest part signifying the pathological whole of being—then Derrida reads Joyce from the other direction. For him, Joyce constitutes the "great memory," a vast software containing all languages and cultures in which the reader's own frame of reference is revealed to be a small and rather insignificant part. Derrida's response to Joyce is therefore ambivalent: on one hand, he defines the "universality" of Joyce in a manner quite distinct from the banal sense of this word in traditional humanist criticism. On the other hand, the overwhelming scope of Joyce's work produces in the reader a certain "admiring resentment," as well as a constant sense of being haunted by the memory of Joyce: not just in the sense of Joyce remembered, but, more disturbingly, in the sense that Joyce's "machine hypermnésique" has always already remembered *us;* our feeble act of reading is contained by it. For Derrida, Joyce is like the absolute Father of Eliot's *Four Quartets* "[t]hat will not leave us, but prevents us everywhere" (1952, 128), except that where Eliot's Father prevents in the specifically theological sense of "going before" as a spiritual guide, Derrida's inescapable Joyce-figure prevents both in this sense and the secular sense of debarring, cutting off, castrating.

The universality of Joyce poses another problem for the reader in that, in its movements toward all-inclusiveness, his text also tends to deny or subvert whatever it affirms, so that every positive meaning in Joyce is subject to self-cancellation, as if written in the mode that Derrida renders as *"sous rature"* (under erasure). Van Boheemen-Saaf cites as an example of this self-deconstructing quality the opening scene of *Ulysses*, where Buck Mulligan's mock Eucharist on the Martello Tower is presented as a profanation of the sacrament, but in such a way as to leave intact certain essential elements of the sacred, thus precluding an interpretation based on the simple opposition sacred/profane. It is the very system of oppositional differences on which literary interpretation is based that Joyce consistently subverts: "the Joycean practice seems an ambivalent move of *both* maintaining *and* invalidating *at once*. In other words, the Joycean text is always "both and," and "or already" (1988, 91).

As in the case of Lacan, Derrida's reading of Joyce relies on a concept of "historicity" that differs from that which is ordinarily invoked in making the charge that poststructuralist criticism is ahistorical and that it fails to examine the circumstances of literary production in terms of its objective, material contexts. Rather, Derrida reminds us that the semantic content of language is historical insofar as linguistic meaning is produced in actual human contexts, and that the signifying function of any expression relies on the history of that expression's use. By exploiting the historically latent forms of signification within every utterance, the Joyce of *Finnegans Wake* produces a "pure historicity" of language, in which

> he tries to make outcrop [*faire affleurer*] with the greatest possible synchrony, at great speed, the greatest power of the meanings buried in each syllabic fragment, subjecting each atom of writing to fission in order to overload the unconscious with the whole memory of man: mythologies, religion, philosophies, sciences, psychoanalysis, literatures. (1984, 149)[1]

This reading offers a way to understand a certain putting into play of the relation between language and history, one which will have consequences for my discussion of the nature of alterity in Joyce.

Returning to the period of literary modernism itself, one finds a critical project that combines the historical grounding of what would come to be "contextual studies" with the illuminations of "theory." The critics of the Frankfurt School might reasonably be said to have been engaged in an ontology of social forms, a deconstruction *avant la lettre* of the experience of modernity. As the work of these critics constitutes an important, if largely implicit, part of the intellectual background for the essays in this volume, I will briefly review some of their contributions to the study of modernity and modern literature.

Georg Simmel's study of the modern city is still of value today, especially as he defines its subjective and somewhat incalculable effects on human relations and consciousness, such as the phenomenon of eccentricity, the cult of originality, and the manifestation of intellectual life as an intensification of the nerve system of urban movement and communication. While being attentive to the facts of urban life, Simmel finds that the city cannot be comprehended by the empirical measures of time and space alone; its material reality, like an accumulating fortune, produces an "unearned increment" of immaterial effects in the realm of individual and collective subjectivity (246). For Simmel, the modern subject is caught in a time lag, overtaken by the events of modernity and by a world where things take place at a speed and on a scale that far surpasses the attempts of the subject to adjust to them. This ever-increasing disparity between the objective world and the interior life of the subject produces a state of permanent anxiety. We live in an age of nervousness (33).

Simmel's observations on the subjective experience of modernity were extended by Walter Benjamin to the realm of literature. In his literary essays, Benjamin is concerned with what he calls "a change in the structure of experience" (1969, 156), an experience that has "fallen in value" (83), that no longer comes into being naturally under modern conditions, and that therefore must be produced synthetically by the artist (157). Benjamin's discussion of the philosophical category of experience (*Erlebnis*) is more essayistic than systematic but is nonetheless valuable for an understanding of literary modernism's relation to modern reality. Benjamin's contribution is, first of all, to historicize the notion of experience, defining it in terms of human life in society rather than in the relation to nature or myth. Second, Benjamin designates a specifically modern function for literature, now entrusted with the synthetic creation of an experience that in itself has lost its traditional value in collective existence as well as in private life.

At this point there is a surprising convergence of the theories of Benjamin and Eliot, two critics ordinarily considered antithetical in every respect. Eliot's background in philosophical idealism puts him at a distinct intellectual and temperamental remove from the sociological concerns and the materialist analyses of the Frankfurt School, but he shares with his German contemporaries a desire to account for the great works of modern literature in terms of a historical moment unprecedented in its hostility to poetry and its destruction of ideal value. Where Benjamin evokes the image of an "inhospitable, blinding age of big-scale industrialism" (1969, 157) from which a modern writer such as Proust seeks refuge in the intimate plenitude of the *mémoire involontaire*, Eliot sees contemporary life as "an immense panorama of futility and anarchy" that can be rendered meaningful only synthetically by art, as in the "mythic method" of Joyce's *Ulysses* (1975, 177). Benjamin would have disputed the necessity of literature's return to myth but would have remained in fundamental agreement with the Eliot of 1922 as to the function of art in giving value to experience. I will discuss how poststructuralist criticism revises this view by affirming a very different relation between art and experience, but for the moment it is worth noting that philosophical discourses on the material reality of history were taking shape simultaneously with the great modernist works of the early twentieth century.

Of all the figures of the Frankfurt School, Theodor Adorno is perhaps the most rigorous in his analysis of modern literature as an effect of the conditions of modernity. Adorno's specific contribution to the study of literature is to demonstrate its inevitable rootedness in contemporary reality, even at those points where its subject matter is turned away from the social or historical. The lyric poem, a form antithetical to the conditions of modern existence, derives its vigor from the very circumstances of this antithesis. Where the modern world is experienced as alien, hostile, and oppressive, this situation is "imprinted in reverse" on the poetic work, whose "distance from mere existence" becomes the measure of what is negative in the latter (40). Unlike lyric poetry, the novel is the literary form traditionally preoccupied with representation of the social order. Adorno shows in the case of Proust, however, the degree to which modernism calls into question the conventions of novelistic representation, with their reassuring qualities of a stable point of view on a more or less coherent object. Though personally respectful of society's norms, Proust as a novelist "suspended its [society's] system of categories and thereby pierced its claim to self-evidence, the illusion that it is part of nature" (176). Proust's irony, however, is not directed simply at social norms but also at those critiques of society that rely too heavily on received ideas. Proust registers a kind of alienation from the alienation of others, a resistance to the more obvious forms of resistance, which produces a completely new relation of the novel to the world of the social (176). In Proust everything, including the category of character or personal identity, is subjected to the transience and contingency of time; his work acquires its authenticity through negativity, that is, through resistance to any kind of positiveness. What Adorno says of Proust is equally true of Joyce: his work ultimately makes its home "on the border where thought too finds its limit" (184).

Adorno thus gestures toward a region beyond thought that is both interior and exterior, both that of the unconscious and that of the modern world evoked by Simmel and Benjamin, an unseizable world "out there," incommensurate in scale and in its infinite transformations to the categories of thought. Joyce's work is full of such gestures toward an unknown inner or outer world: the dark "journey westward" toward the "grey impalpable world" of the dead (D 225); the "reality of experience" to be encountered only "away from home and friends" (P 225); the final black point that marks the limit of interrogation in "Ithaca" (U 17.2332); and in *Finnegans Wake*, where the form of language itself is pushed to this limit, the tenuous, undecidable relation between "every person, place and thing in the chaosmos of Alle" and Joyce's "variously inflected, differently pronounced, otherwise spelled, changeably meaning vocable scriptsigns" (FW 118.21–28).

Adorno's observations help us to conceive of literary modernism as more than a series of technical innovations; more than a preoccupation with image, myth, and consciousness; and finally more than simply a response to the alienating effects of modernity. From Conrad through Proust, Joyce, Eliot, Woolf, Kafka, Stevens, and Beckett, the distinctive project of modernism is the encounter with *otherness* variously conceived or marked as beyond conception. The apparent innovations of modernism—what Eliot calls the "dislocation" of language into meaning (1975, 65)—are the formal consequences of this willed encounter. In his brief and dazzling essay "The Other in Proust," Emmanuel Lévinas accounts for the remarkably self-generating power of Proust's language by its continuing preoccupation with the mystery of the self—experienced as other—and therefore with the mystery of the self's relation to the world. Proust's narrator is in a sense never himself; he stands to one side of himself; his emotion is always "the emotion of emotions," emotion aroused by reflection on emotion, as if felt in some Platonic cave of affect. Proust is a novelist of social reality not because he depicts the manners of his age, but rather because his narrator's emotion exists through others—Albertine, his grandmother, his own past self—and in this way it retains its alterity (163). Here as elsewhere, Lévinas has little patience for the philosophical or the political idealism that desperately seeks to abolish alterity through either the appropriating strategies of knowledge or the dream of a social collectivity based on complete mutual understanding. Proust's virtue lies in leaving the other intact while maintaining his fascination with its very quality of alterity. His lesson consists in "situating reality in a relation which remains for ever other, with the Other as absence and mystery" (165).

The alterity that Proust locates primarily in the self is extended through other modernist works—and especially those by Joyce—to the world at large in a manner that surpasses the familiar phenomenon of alienation. Deep within the labyrinth of *Finnegans Wake*, a chapter (III.3) is devoted to the interrogation of the book's principal figure, HCE, by the "four old men" who bear occasional resemblance to the four evangelists of the New Testament. One of these worthies makes an allusion to Proust ("the prouts") as "the poeta" who invents writing as a "raiding" (*FW* 482.31–32), language that echoes Eliot's characterization in *Four Quartets* of his own poetical work as "a raid on the inarticulate" (1952, 128). The object of this raiding—both reading and writing—in Proust's case as well as Eliot's is the other both within and without, the alterity of the self and its uncanny relation to the objective world, or in Lacanian terms, to the real. The limits to thought imposed by this alterity mark an end point, a "point of eschatology" (*FW* 482.33) that, as the theological term implies, exists in a historical dimension as well and that constitutes the object of Joyce's own profaned gospel: "That's the point of eschatology our book of kills reaches for now in soandso many counterpoint words" (*FW* 482.33–34). Joyce writes his own murdered version of the gospel set forth in the eighth-century Irish Book of Kells; his "book of kills," however, is aimed at an eschatological goal located not in the future Second Coming of Christ but rather in the limits to thought and thus to language set by the contemporary experience of history. Joyce's profaned evangelist conveys the structure of this history as a vertiginous elaboration of Giambattista Vico's theory of historical return, or *ricorso:* "Now, the doctrine obtains, we have occasioning cause causing effects and affects occasionally recausing alter-effects" (*FW* 482.36–483.1). Rabaté reads this passage as referring to the peculiar nature of language in *Finnegans Wake*, where a kind of "feedback" distorts the cause and effect of linguistic sequence and thus the signifying function of language (1984, 79). To these observations on linguistic structure, however, I would add that Joyce is speaking historically and not only in the transhistorical mode suggested by Vico; Joyce also alludes to the pressure on his language produced by the particular reality of the historical moment, to the fate of a literary language that would reflect the uncanny effects and affects of alterity as they are produced in the surrounding world: "altereffects."

Here I return to Derrida's remark on the "pure historicity" (1984, 149) of *Finnegans Wake*, of a language that, through its extreme condensation and synchrony of meanings, purifies itself of adulteration by the ideological and epistemological constructs of history, those determining constraints that make history a nightmare from which Stephen Dedalus tries to awake (*U* 2.377). Rodolphe Gasché compares this observation of Derrida's to an earlier discussion in which the philosopher claims, in writing his monumental work *Glas*, to have deliberately relinquished a measure of responsibility for the control and mastery of his language. A text written in this manner creates effects that are "absolutely non-anticipatable, out of sight." Gasché finds this "desire to open writing to unforeseeable effects, in other words, to the Other," to be very much in the spirit of Joyce. It is a writing that "calculates with the incalculable" (230). This "openness to the arrival of the Other" has specific consequences for the form of Joyce's writing: "it is singular, untranslatable, affirming the chance of encounters and the randomness of coincidences." It cannot afford the security of unconditional affirmation.

Instead, what Joyce affirms is precisely that which remains in doubt, that which cannot be calculated and resists meaning. In the course of writing his major works, Joyce produces a language that increasingly creates the effect of having been released to the aleatory drift of objects and events, thus achieving a more authentic historicity than one which, in Pound's ironic phrase, keeps pace with "the march of events" (61). This view of Joyce is close to Lévinas's view of Proust, with the difference that Joyce reserves no special place for the self in the incalculable world to which his work opens up. From this perspective, Joyce's relation to his historical moment is quite different from that claimed for him by Eliot. Eliot sees the method of *Ulysses* as one of "controlling, of ordering, of giving a shape and a significance" to the anarchy of contemporary history (1975, 177). Where Eliot sees mere anarchy, poststructuralist criticism sees rather the strangeness of a modern life that can no longer be securely mastered by thought. Matthew Arnold's was the last literary generation to have attempted to see life "steadily" and see it "whole" (67). Instead, Joyce's work is distinguished by its openness to the risks implied in acknowledging the alterity of the other. It is important to recognize this aspect of Joyce as a corrective to the critical tradition that sees in the encyclopedic character of his work a kind of totalizing knowledge. Against the Arnoldian ideal of seeing life steadily and whole, and notwithstanding the master narratives of Homer and Vico, Joyce offers a wavering gaze directed or indirected toward a wobbling universe experienced in its multiple aspects but not in its totality. Like the alleged indecency in Mansion House Park performed by HCE, the world appears in Joyce as "admittedly an incautious but, at its wildest, a partial exposure" (FW 34.26).

The "scene" of modernity evoked in the title of this volume refers to a modern tradition that conceives of contemporary history as something seen: Whitman's "democratic vistas," Arnold's "seeing life whole," James's *American Scene*, Eliot's "vast panorama," Pound's image, and Leopold Bloom's "final meditation" on the ultimate advertisement, "not exceeding the span of casual vision and congruous with the velocity of modern life" (U 592.1772–73). The scene of modernity includes the spectacle of imperial power as manifested in parades and exhibitions, as well as the visual space of the modern city, widened and straightened by Haussmann, elevated and rationalized by modern architecture, synchronized and accelerated by the rhythms of labor, production, commerce, and mass transportation. Modernity has its inner scenes as well, producing effects of anxiety, nervousness, fantasy, and the uncanny within the individual psyche. Joyce's work casts its eye on these various prospects of the age, rendering them with sympathy, with irony, and with a penetrating analytical power.

The notion of alterity, specifically as it applies to the effects of modernity, serves as the other sign under which the essays in this volume are gathered. The first three essays address the effects of certain forms of power and knowledge characteristic of the early twentieth century: colonial domination, nationalism, and anthropology. The elements of alterity belonging to these institutions are suggested in Lacan's theory of *le grand Autre* (the big Other), meaning the social order, or as Slavoj Žižek puts it, "the symbolic texture that constitutes the social bond" (1993, 235). But they are also suggested in another way by Michel Foucault's conception of power as multiple, mobile, and ultimately unstable (1980b, 102). Foucault alludes to an incalculable dimension of power, a feedback effect that works against its primary dominating force. Chapter 1, "Colonial Spaces in Joyce's Dublin," explores this feedback effect in the nature of the British imperial presence, as this presence figures in Joyce's first three major works of fiction. Here, where imperialism takes concrete form in architectural space, Joyce is concerned with the unpredictable effects of subversion, irony, and indifference that power provokes. The essential incoherence of colonial domination is dramatized by the scene in which the viceregal cavalcade progresses through the streets of the Irish capital to a heterogeneous and heterodox series of reactions from the citizenry. The other of colonial power—that which remains unmastered by it because beyond its conception—is finally personified by the mysterious figure in the brown macintosh, a figure that I identify with Joyce himself.

If Irish nationalism is a principal force of resistance to British colonial domination, it is also a form of repression in its treatment of Jews and others designated as foreigners in Ireland. The paradox that combines national liberation with nationalist repression is addressed in chapter 2, "The Comedy of Intolerance in Proust and Joyce," which compares the anti-Semitism of the Sinn Fein movement to that of the Dreyfus affair in France. Anti-Semitism is by definition a preoccupation with otherness, but beyond the obvious fact that it constitutes the Jew as other, I find relevant here Žižek's notion of nationalist fantasy as symptomatic of an anxiety over the possession of enjoyment. Starting from Lacan's thesis that enjoyment is always "the enjoyment of the Other"—that is, something one covets as belonging rightfully to oneself but which is in the possession of the other—he argues that this "theft" in fact represents one's own relationship to enjoyment, which is characterized by a fear of excess. It follows that "the hatred of the Other is the hatred of our own excess of enjoyment" (1993, 206). This theory is pertinent to an understanding of nationalistic xenophobia, which sees its object as enjoying something to which it is not entitled. In Proust, the Jews are suspected of enjoying the privileges of French citizenship without being willing to obey the patriotic "call to duty" in a time of national crisis. In Joyce, Leopold Bloom is suspected of just about everything, from refusing to share his supposed winnings in the Ascot Cup to getting "drunk as a boiled owl" (U 12.510) and riding home in a cab—in short of enjoying to excess the objects of his persecutors' own fantasies.

In both writers, however, the analysis of this situation is rendered problematic—and comic—by a certain dissonance of alternate narrative registers. Joyce especially undermines the conventional reliability of a uniform narrative voice, so that parts of his work seem narrated by a voice alien to the implied contract that allows the reader to identify with a coherent subject position in the narrator. The comic anarchy of narrative registers seems designed to demonstrate that every such position is susceptible to a swerve into something other than itself.

In chapter 3, "Anthropologies of Modernism: Joyce, Eliot, Lévy-Bruhl,"

I turn from colonialism and nationalism to the shifting senses of alterity that arise from the uneasy relation between anthropology and literary modernism. Lucien Lévy-Bruhl's studies of mystical intuition in "primitive mentality" were important to modernism for their scientific legitimation of an alternative mode of perception, a cultural other to modern reason. This theory resonates with Eliot's notion that poetry has its origins in a primitive unity of culture and consciousness, as defined both historically and in terms of the poet's mind. His idea of the primitive as the unified source of poetry contrasts with his representation of the Jew as an alien, disruptive element in the cultural order. The mythologizing gestures inherent in both the positions of Lévy-Bruhl and Eliot are satirized in Joyce, who implicitly identifies the Jew as cultural other with the spirit of literature. Anticipating Blanchot, Joyce demonstrates his affinity with the nomadic aspect of Jewishness, the condition of being exiled, on the move, at or beyond the limits of a pagan, rooted experience. Alterity is shown to be an essential condition of the literary project in which Joyce is engaged.

The next two chapters treat the alienating effects of modernity itself, apart from its specific manifestations in institutions of power and knowledge. Here, the historical conditions of modernity are seen as the background to the decay of artistic mimesis and to the experience of reading as a dying art. Although these crises are commonly represented in terms of aesthetic loss, they in fact point to radical changes in the function of literature as mediating between a bewildering, unprecedented social reality and the subjectivity of the reading public, or what Adorno calls the "collective undercurrent" in the name of which the poet, or writer, speaks (45).

Chapter 4, "Joyce, *Hamlet*, Mallarmé," documents a modern crisis of mimesis. For Mallarmé, Hamlet is the archetypal figure of alienation, whose estrangement extends to the state of his own being. A "stranger everywhere," in Mallarmé's words, Hamlet is also the perfect representation of what Lacan terms the *sujet barré*, the subject who exists by virtue of the negativity of his own subjecthood. The problem for the actor playing Hamlet, then, is how to interpret a character who is both there and not there, a mere ghost of his ghostly father. Mallarmé finds the solution to this problem of artistic representation in the performance of the famous actor Mounet-Sully, who brings a particularly faded and spectral quality to the role. In Stephen Dedalus's informal lecture on Shakespeare at the National Library of Ireland, he borrows from Mallarmé while also insisting on the ghostly nature of the playwright, identifying Shakespeare not with Hamlet, as is usually done, but with the ghost of Hamlet's father. The treatment of the play in both modern writers can be understood in terms of Benjamin's theory of the decay of mimesis, according to which art has lost its traditional object of imitation in the truth of the *logos* and now can only strive to represent the absence of this object, which nonetheless retains its haunting power.

The "fading" of mimesis witnessed here corresponds to certain changes in the nature of reading, at least as this practice is portrayed in works of literature. Chapter 5, "Scenes of Reading," records a crisis in the representation of reading: traditionally seen as a kind of participation in a relatively unified cultural or national formation, the act of reading is represented in twentieth-century writing as more solitary, more heterogeneous, and more ephemeral than ever before. Once again it is instructive to compare Joyce with Proust, the other great writer of the century. For Proust, reading is a very private act, allowing the reader to receive communication from the other while preserving the solitude and the intellectual power that are compromised by actual conversation. For Joyce, reading also involves a relation to the other, but this other is variously conceived: on one hand, it is constituted by the heterogeneous textuality of modernity itself; on the other hand, by the unconscious. Thus it is that the ideal reader of *Finnegans Wake* is an ideal insomniac, poring over the oniric matter of the unconscious while nonetheless retaining the wakefulness one otherwise loses on entering that shadowy realm.

The last two chapters turn to Joyce's final work, the one that resonates most strongly with the reverberation of differing linguistic effects. In contrast to a history of *Wake* studies that have tended to focus either on mythic narratives or on the pure play of language, these essays are designed to show the degree to which Joyce's last work is rooted in historical contexts while yet retaining its openness to alterity. Joyce's achievement in the *Wake* cannot be adequately appreciated solely in terms of the language of the text. Rather, Joyce is demonstrating through his work the linguistic texture of history; that is, that historical events signify with all of the ambiguity and the unpredictable effects of language, and that history takes place *in* language, occurring within the space of language insofar as it has any meaning at all.

With chapter 6, "Fatal Signatures: Forgery and Colonization in *Finnegans Wake*," I return to the scene of colonial domination addressed in the first essay of this volume. Only here, however, the unintended effects of subversion and irony produced by the forces of power are multiplied beyond measure. Joyce's treatment of the "trial" of Charles Stewart Parnell for his alleged complicity in the Phoenix Park murders of 1882 simply destabilizes any single reading of this event. Instead, the famous forged letter used in an attempt to incriminate Parnell becomes the point of departure for a reflection on the ambiguity, ambivalence, and instability of every possible meaning the trial could have, either for the forces of British domination or for those of Irish national liberation, forces that themselves, moreover, are shown to be not entirely distinct from one another. Joyce's language effectively collapses the distinction between forgery and authenticity, as well as a number of other conceptual oppositions on which the exercise of power rests. All of these are exploded in the *Wake*'s controlled anarchy of laughter.

This strategy of comic subversion nonetheless offers insight into the nature of history as Joyce conceives it. The traditional model for interpretations of *Finnegans Wake* is based on Joyce's allusions to Vico, who proposes the eternal recurrence of a four-part cycle of history. Vico's myth of history in fact serves the same function in *Finnegans Wake* that the *Odyssey* serves in *Ulysses:* that of an overall skeletal framework that takes the place of traditional narrative structure. Neither of these mythic frameworks, however, is of much use in understanding Joyce's treatment of specific historical events, and that is why I suggest a revision in the interpretive model that relies exclusively on Vico for understanding the nature of history in the *Wake.* In his representation of historical situations such as the Parnell affair or the British presence in India, Joyce's model of history strikes me as closer to Althusser's theory of structural causality, which denies the presence of some principle external to historical events themselves—a principle that, according to traditional theories of history, ultimately determines the course of events. Instead, as Jameson explains this theory, "the whole existence of the structure consists of its effects, in short. . . . the structure, which is merely a specific combination of particular elements, is nothing outside its effects" (1981, 24–25). Such a reading of history I find to be entirely compatible with Joyce's representation of history as a somewhat aleatory, deeply equivocal, and always ambivalent proliferation of signifying effects.

The final chapter, "Writing in the *Wake* of Empire," demonstrates this proliferation through a study of Joyce's parody of colonial discourse, especially as it refers to the often revisited incident of HCE's alleged indecency in the bushes of Phoenix Park. Here the discourse of colonization, whether in Ireland or in India, is penetrated by male sexual fantasies in a way that exposes both the erotic formations of empire and the imperialist dimensions of masculine desire. As parody, Joyce's text renders comically manifest the duplicity of the discourse of power, a doubleness that has been expressed in several ways. For Freud, it is the presence of two distinct psychic motives in all language: one that attempts to take account of reality, the other that expresses desire. For Derrida, it is the phenomenon of "double writing," which occurs when writing goes back over itself with "an indecidable stroke" (1981, 143). For the postcolonial theorist Homi Bhabha, it is the splitting and disfigurement of the voice of authority confronted with the intractable presence of the uncolonized other (1990, 313), creating for colonial authority a host of uncanny, unmanageable effects such as mimicry and sabotage. *Finnegans Wake*, and to a great extent all of Joyce's work, may be seen precisely as a series of acts of sabotage from within the structures that make of language an instrument of power, be it political, historical, or literary. Joyce achieves this by opening up within those structures the space of the uncolonized, unrepresented, and incalculable: the space of the other.

1

Colonial Spaces in Joyce's Dublin

For ten years at the beginning of the twentieth century, James Joyce lived in Trieste, a city that shared many qualities with his native Dublin. Both cities had ancient and distinctive identities, both were Catholic, both were dominated by a foreign power, and both celebrated indigenous languages radically different from those of their conquerors. They were both colonial cities. When, in 1907, Joyce lectured at the Università Popolare on "Ireland, Island of Saints and Sages," his audience would have been quick to see the parallels between Dublin and Trieste, including that between Irish nationalism and the Irredentist movement against Austria.

The Triestines' natural receptiveness to the theme of colonial domination would have encouraged Joyce, for example, in his comparison of British rule in Ireland to "what the Belgian has done in the Congo Free State" (*CW* 166), a subject of international scandal in those days.[1] Joyce's language is liveliest, however, when describing the effects of imperial presence within the space of the Irish capital. As evidence of the "moral separation" between England and Ireland, Joyce recalls never having heard the English hymn "God Save the King" sung in public "without a storm of hisses, shouts, and shushes that made the solemn and majestic music absolutely inaudible." When an English monarch wishes to visit Ireland, he notes,

> there is always a lively flurry to persuade the mayor to receive him at the gates of the city. But, in fact, the last monarch who entered [Edward VII in 1903] had to be content with an informal reception by the sheriff, since the mayor had refused the honour. (*CW* 163)

What interests me here is the way Joyce conceives of the city as a contested space of imperfectly accomplished colonial domination. With its broad vistas, ordered arrangement, and masterful architecture, the modern city is the ideal site for the display and deployment of imperial authority.

But it is also a space in which that authority produces uncontrolled and to some degree unpredictable effects of resistance. In its formal boundaries and its arrangement of structures into linear but irregular patterns, the space of the city may be compared to that of the literary text, where authorial control is continually subverted both by the constraints and by the unintended effects of language.

In the discussion that follows, I draw on representations of Dublin from Joyce's first three major works in order to explore what I call "spaces of colonial authority." In architectural parlance, a space of authority is one physically dominated by an imposing structure in such a way that it extends the area of that domination, like the gardens of the Palace of Versailles. In addition to this purely physical notion of spatial authority, I consider both its political dimension and its effects on the subjective consciousness of the city dweller. In doing so I am consciously following the work of Michel Foucault on the spatial distribution of power, both in systematic inquiries such as *Discipline and Punish* and in informal interviews such as the one in which he states, "A whole history remains to be written of *spaces*—which would at the same time be the history of *powers* . . .— from the great strategies of geo-politics to the little tactics of the habitat" (1980a, 149). One might add Foucault's observation that beginning with the eighteenth century, "one sees the development of reflection on architecture as a function of the aims and techniques of the government of societies" (1984, 239). Although Foucault is thinking primarily of French architecture, his observation applies with particular force to the case of Dublin, where most of the institutional buildings were erected during the eighteenth century in order literally to solidify Protestant rule over a fairly hostile and intractable Catholic population.

In Joyce's case, subjective consciousness is often defined in terms of a spatial environment created both by the myriad forces of modernity and by the specific system of authority represented by the British imperial presence in Ireland at the turn of the twentieth century. For Joyce, British domination is part of both the architectural and the subjective environments; both architectural space and the space of consciousness are sites of a continual struggle among the competing claims of individual freedom, nationalist aspirations, and imperial authority. Joyce's work thus tends to represent the city in terms of the contradictions that are in fact embodied in urban space. On one hand, the architecture and planning of Dublin—the work of official bodies such as the Wide Streets Commission and the Royal Institute of Architects—forms a concrete expression of modern colonial domination. On the other hand, Joyce is very much alive to the city as the space of subjective freedom and the scene of subversion, deflection, irony, ambivalence, mimicry, indifference—in short, to all of the various effects of modernity that compromise what would otherwise be the unitary and singular nature of authority.

*   *   *

Among the many suggestive renderings of city space in Joyce's *Dubliners,* I wish to single out a passage from the final section of the short story that completes this collection, "The Dead." The passage occurs at the end of the annual New Year's dance held by two elderly sisters, Kate and Julia Morkan, at their "dark gaunt house on Usher's Island" (*D* 175), a drab section of the Dublin quayside just east of the industrial complex occupied by the Guinness brewery. Well after midnight Gabriel Conroy, his wife, Gretta, and two other guests bid their hostesses goodnight and emerge onto the quayside:

> The morning was still dark. A dull yellow light brooded over the houses and the river; and the sky seemed to be descending. It was slushy underfoot: and only streaks and patches of snow lay on the roofs, on the parapets of the quay and on the area railings. The lamps were still burning redly in the murky air and, across the river, the palace of the Four Courts stood out menacingly against the heavy sky. (*D* 214)

In a manner already explored by figures like Poe and Baudelaire, Joyce establishes an analogy between the oppressive urban landscape and the psychology of the subject. The darkness and heaviness of the air make for a sense of brooding, while architectural elements such as railings and parapets add to the feeling of confinement. The paragraph, which is written from Gabriel's point of view, resonates with his subjective experience. At the party, Gabriel has been taunted by Miss Ivors, a colleague from the university, for his indifference to the nationalist cause and to the Irish cultural revival, which for her involves learning the Irish language and taking trips to the West of Ireland, home of an ostensibly more primitive and indigenous Irish people. Stung by Miss Ivors's accusation that he is a "West Briton"—that is, an Irishman who considers his country part of Britain—he says suddenly, "O, to tell you the truth, [. . .] I'm sick of my own country, sick of it!" (*D* 190)

1. Palace of the Four Courts. Lawrence Collection No. Royal 1655. Reprinted courtesy of the National Library of Ireland.

For the promoters of the Irish revival, the Irish language and the Irish-speaking peasants of the West are signs of an original, national purity that is symbolically constructed as an ideological defense against British domination and, more generally, against the effects of modernization created by an increasingly urban and industrial environment. Gabriel's heated retort, however, reacts to the confining effects of an ideology that raises objections to his trip to the continent and to his cultivation of European languages at the expense of "your own language . . . Irish" (D 189). His impatience with this aspect of Irish nationalism reflects Joyce's own interrogations in the Trieste lecture, delivered in the same year that he was writing "The Dead":

> What race, or what language . . . can boast of being pure today? And no race has less right to utter such a boast than the race now living in Ireland. Nationality (if it really is not a convenient fiction like so many others to which the scalpels of present-day scientists have given the coup de grâce) must find its reason for being rooted in something that surpasses and transcends and informs changing things like blood and the human word. (CW 165–66)

The idea that nationality might find its reason for being in the transcendent power of art is hardly dreamt of in Gabriel's philosophy, but he nonetheless gives voice to Joyce's skepticism of a national revival based on notions of racial and linguistic purity.

To return to the early morning scene on the quayside, the confining atmosphere of the city serves as an exterior manifestation of Gabriel's "sickness"—the paralysis of a subject trapped between the narrow-minded demands of nationalist sentiment and the profoundly oppressive effects of colonial domination. As a symbol of the latter, Joyce has chosen the "menacing" aspect of the Palace of the Four Courts, built by the British architect James Gandon in the 1790s (fig. 1). A protégé of John Beresford, the Unionist politician nicknamed "King of Ireland" for his powers of patronage, Gandon had earlier built the imposing Custom House over the protests of the republican leader Napper Tandy, who led a crowd armed with adzes and shovels in an attempt to wreck the new construction (Craig 240). The Palace of the Four Courts housed the central law courts of Ireland (Chancery, King's Bench, Common Pleas, and the Exchequer) and was built in a style of Roman grandeur reflective of judicial authority. Its most distinctive feature is a huge domed drum-tower, seventy-six feet in diameter, rising above massive orders of columns, pilasters, and porticoes in gray granite. In the great central hall there stood a series of colossal statues representing, respectively, Punishment, Eloquence, Mercy, Prudence, Law, Wisdom, Justice, and Liberty; in the walls above were eight panels depicting the history of British rule in Ireland from the time of Henry II. During the rising of the United Irishmen in 1798, the palace was seen as the ultimate manifestation of the Protestant Ascendancy's self-confidence. In the Civil War of 1922–23 it was seized by Irish Republican Army troops who destroyed the panels and statues.

The menacing appearance of the Palace of the Four Courts is over-determined by its domineering architectural form, by its place in a history of colonial violence, and, in the context of *Dubliners*, by a more far-reaching repression internal to Irish society. Joyce tells his Trieste audience that economic and intellectual conditions in Ireland prevent the development of individuality, that "the soul of the country . . . is paralysed by the influence and admonitions of the church, while its body is manacled by the police, the tax office, and the garrison" (*CW* 171). This endemic paralysis colors the very landscape of the city.

In Joyce's story, however, the bleak scene on the quay is followed by Gabriel's memory of a series of privileged moments from his life with

Gretta. All of these are drawn from city life and seem to depend on the urban setting for their particular form of happiness:

> They were standing on the crowded platform and he was placing a ticket inside the warm palm of her glove. He was standing with her in the cold, looking in through a grated window at a man making bottles in a roaring furnace. (*D* 214)

For Gabriel these are "moments of ecstasy" that he longs to recall to his wife, "to make her forget the years of their dull existence together" (*D* 215).

At such moments Joyce shows that for the modern subject the city is a space of enjoyment as well as confinement and regulation. One of the conclusions to be drawn from Walter Benjamin's studies in urban modernity is that, as people become more objectified and their time more commodified in public life, there is a corresponding value placed on the individual's private and subjective experience. Private living space, for example, becomes for the first time the antithesis of the work space: "The private person who squares his accounts with reality in his office demands that the [private] interior be maintained in his illusions" (1986, 154). By the same token, the depersonalizing environment of the crowd or of industrial production creates, paradoxically, occasions for extraordinary moments of private fantasy and intimacy. Gabriel's intimate contact with Gretta's gloved hand is savored all the more for taking place on a crowded train platform; his feelings of tenderness are heightened precisely by their quality of inner refuge from the noise of the glassmaker's furnace. In these moments that "no one knew of or would ever hear of," treasured and concealed like jewels in a box, Joyce registers the fetishization of privacy as a condition of modern urban existence.

One of the many ironies of Joyce's story is that Gabriel's moments of intimacy with his wife have the quality of an illusion; they are not shared by Gretta, who is absorbed in her own memory of a lost love that has nothing to do with her husband and their "dull existence together." The oppressive presence of the Four Courts thus has its counterpart in this marriage, whose conditions have led Gretta to conceal from her jealous and somewhat pompous husband the memory of a young man who loved her long ago and, as she believes, died for her.

It is no accident that the setting of this long-repressed memory is the West of Ireland, which earlier in the story has been established, for the purposes of the Irish revival, as an almost mythic realm of cultural and

linguistic authenticity. It is equally clear to me, however, that the passionate invocation of Michael Furey's memory enacted by Gretta's confession
cannot be likened to Miss Ivors's insistent patronage of the West. Here my
reading departs from those who equate in political terms the scene of
Gretta's memory with the romantic "Irishness" celebrated by Miss Ivors.[2]
On the contrary, it seems that Joyce has juxtaposed these two evocations of
the West precisely in order to show the difference between a strident,
somewhat hollow political discourse and a narrative so deeply personal
that it acquires universal significance. I intend here not to recuperate
Joyce's story for an apolitical modernist aesthetic but rather to enforce
Joyce's own distinction between a superficial nationalism of "frigid enthu-
siasts" (CW 173) and a more profound sense of nationality that transcends
ideas of blood and language (CW 166).

For Joyce, British domination is only an accessory to Ireland's self-in-
duced paralysis of the spirit. The "gradual reawakening of the Irish conscience" (CW 169) will come only by allowing for the return of the repressed, as Gretta does in her tearful story. This is a political act insofar as
it liberates her, however momentarily, from the possessive compulsions of
Gabriel, who also experiences in this evidence of his own reduced stature a
feeling of release from the role of domineering husband: "It hardly pained
him now to think how poor a part he, her husband, had played in her life"
(D 223). "His own identity was fading out into a grey impalpable world:
the solid world itself which these dead had one time reared and lived in was
dissolving and dwindling" (D 224–25).

This solid world is, among other things, the concrete environment of
the urban landscape that loses its distinctive qualities as Gabriel's own begin to fade, as if his identity along with his feeling of entrapment within it
somehow depended on the material solidity of his surroundings. This con-
cluding scene takes place in the Conroys' room at the Gresham Hotel,
which faces west across Sackville Street, so that when Gabriel turns to the
window, we may see him facing, in fact, westward:

> A few light taps upon the pane made him turn to the window. It had
> begun to snow again. He watched sleepily the flakes, silver and dark,
> falling obliquely against the lamplight. The time had come for him to
> set out on his journey westward. (D 223)

The quality of the urban landscape is completely different here from what
it has been earlier in the story: it is a space defined neither by authority nor
by the hoarded pleasures of private enjoyment. The falling snow, which is

general over Ireland, joins the city with the natural landscapes extending to the west: "the dark central plain . . . the treeless hills . . . the Bog of Allen, and farther westward, . . . the dark mutinous Shannon waves." This final evocation of the West transcends the kind of enthusiasm represented in Miss Ivors and aligns itself with the inescapable feeling of loss represented in Gretta's story. In its effacement of oppositions—of Irish and British, country and city, traditional and modern, West of Ireland and "West Britain"—it offers release from difference, but only in the sense that death offers release from the discord of life. In keeping with the spirit of *Dubliners* as a whole, the end of the story finds neither resolution nor compensation for the oppressive and alienating features of political and personal life. Rather, it finds deliverance from these conditions only in an elegiac mode, only in thoughts of death.

*   *   *

In *A Portrait of the Artist as a Young Man,* subjective experience is again conditioned by structures of colonial domination that take concrete form in the space of Dublin. In the famous conclusion to chapter 4, Stephen Dedalus consecrates his future to art while moving literally offshore, distancing himself as far as possible from the city by walking out onto the northern breakwall and into the tides of Dublin harbor. In the following and final chapter, however, he is back in the center of the city, tracing a familiar route between his home and University College, the institution opened in 1854 for middle-class Catholic students like him. On the way he passes the more prestigious Trinity College, attended by the sons of wealthy and powerful Protestants:

> The grey block of Trinity on his left, set heavily in the city's ignorance like a great dull stone set in a cumbrous ring, pulled his mind downward; and while he was striving this way and that to free his feet from the fetters of the reformed conscience he came upon the droll statue of the national poet of Ireland. He looked at it without anger: for, though sloth of the body and of the soul crept over it like unseen vermin, over the shuffling feet and around the servile head, it seemed humbly conscious of its indignity. (*P* 194)

Stephen's passage along College Green Street allows for the ironic juxtaposition of two very different monuments that are nonetheless closely

2. Trinity College, west façade. Lawrence Collection No. Royal 4717. Reprinted courtesy of the National Library of Ireland.

related in the logic of this narrative. Trinity College is originally an Eliza-bethan institution, built in 1592 on land granted to the citizens of Dublin for their loyalty during a rebellion. Stephen walks past the buildings sur-rounding its west court, which were rebuilt in 1759 under the provostship of Francis Andrews, an accomplished courtier and member of parliament, which paid for the reconstruction. The western façade of this complex stands at the head of Dame Street, facing Dublin Castle at the other end. As the architectural historian Maurice Craig writes, Trinity "remains the most ample piece of collegiate architecture in these [British] islands, planned on the heroic scale in one of the most commanding sites of Dub-lin" (180) (fig. 2). In its classical form it stands as an architectural counter-part to the Four Courts and to the Bank of Ireland (the former Parliament House) across the street. It is a symbolic counterpart as well, for just as in the nineteenth century the Four Courts and Dublin Castle were the seats of Protestant rule, Trinity College was the intellectual heart of the Ascendancy. For most of its history Trinity excluded Catholics; in Joyce's time it was regarded as especially "foreign" because of its hostility to the Irish revival (Deane 308).

Stephen fails to appreciate the heroic classicism of Trinity; instead he sees it as a "great dull stone" whose weight has both social and psychological effects, oppressing the surrounding urban environment as well as his own mind. To him it stands as an institution of privilege and dull learning amid the city's general ignorance, as if the hallowed traditions of Trinity were no more enlightened or enlightening than the surrounding masses of unlettered Dubliners. Stephen feels its confining presence in body as well as mind; as he walks across the space commanded by Trinity College, the "reformed conscience" of Trinity's Protestantism produces fetters from which he must strive "this way and that to free his feet."[3]

In the shadow of Trinity's west façade stands the statue of Thomas Moore (fig. 3), to Stephen, Ireland's "national poet" only in an ironic sense. Author of the popular *Irish Melodies* (1808–34), Moore is represented here as a conscious fraud, serving the interests of power by capitalizing on the most sentimental ideas of Irishness in poems with titles like "Let Erin Remember the Days of Old," "Oh, the Shamrock," and "How Oft has the Banshee Cried." Like most of Moore's work, the *Melodies* were dedicated to aristocratic members of the Ascendancy. A poem entitled "The Meeting of the Waters" opens with these lines:

> There is not in the wide world a valley so sweet
> As that vale in whose bosom the bright waters meet;
> Oh! the last rays of feeling and life must depart,
> Ere the bloom of that valley shall fade from my heart.
> (184)

In *Ulysses,* Leopold Bloom crosses under the same statue of Moore in College Green and reflects on the fact that it stands over a public urinal:

> He crossed under Tommy Moore's roguish finger. They did right to put him up over a urinal: meeting of the waters. (*U* 8.414–15)

Stephen, however, has a different view of the statue. For him, it stands in direct relation to the grey block of Trinity, a symbol of the way Ireland has embraced its own ignorance and worshiped its own "sorrowful legend" (*P* 195) in such a way as to satisfy the complacent feelings of superiority sheltered within Trinity's walls. The statue, moreover, destabilizes the idea of authentic Irishness that Moore's poetry does so much to celebrate.

3. Statue of Thomas Moore. Lawrence Collection No. Imperial 2513. Reprinted courtesy of the National Library of Ireland.

Stephen's image of Moore's servile form as "a Firbolg in the borrowed cloak of a Milesian" (*P* 194) evokes the names of two early Irish peoples. In Irish tradition the Firbolgs were short, dark people, among the most primitive inhabitants of ancient Ireland. The Milesians, descendants of the Spanish knight Milesius, conquered Ireland in 1300 B.C., and are regarded as more civilized than the Firbolgs. Stephen is saying that the figure of Moore with his sentimental verses merely "borrows the cloak" of a poet, and that in reality he stands for a baser instinct, the "grossness of intelligence," the "bluntness of feeling" of the rude Firbolg mind (*P* 195). At the same time, however, the rhetorical opposition of Firbolg and Milesian disrupts the essential notion of Irishness and exposes it as divided in its very origin or, at the very least, as something owing its cultural value to foreign invasion, by Milesians and later by Danes, Normans, and Anglo-Saxons—all of whom, as Joyce points out in his Trieste lecture, contribute to the makeup of the modern Irish people (*CW* 166). Although in that lecture Joyce calls this race a "new entity," he cannot escape the suggestion that whatever is valued as most "Irish" is bound to be, paradoxically, the result of foreign invasion when it is not a merely sentimental fiction. In such

ways Joyce destabilizes not just the notion of Irishness but also the familiar opposition between colonizer and colonized.

A similar complexity applies to the literary construction of urban space,
which figures alternately as a restraining presence and a stimulant to sense
and imagination. The grey block of Trinity may weigh on Stephen's spirit,
but the neighboring statue of Moore gives rise to a more irritated reflection on Stephen's friend Davin, the peasant student whose unthinking
obedience to a Fenian ideal rejects "whatsoever of thought or a feeling
came to him from England or by way of English culture" (P 196). This tacit
recognition of England's contribution to Stephen's own imaginative life is
compromised, however, by the sudden appearance of a flower-seller from
whom Stephen must flee "before she offered her ware to another, a tourist
from England or a student at Trinity" (P 199)—that is, one who, unlike
Stephen, had money to buy her flowers. Thus the chance encounters of
street life in Dublin lead alternately to the acknowledgment of British cultural value and to a sense of exclusion from the privileges of British economic power.

*   *   *

Literary modernism has been called an art of cities, meaning that it is produced in cities, that cities are its natural habitat, and that modernist works
are largely about the city and its effects on human consciousness. No other
writer, however, thematizes the city the way Joyce does in *Ulysses*, and of
all the episodes in that book, chapter 10 is the most explicitly devoted to
the exploration and representation of urban space. "Wandering Rocks" is
arranged in the form of nineteen separate scenes of ordinary life in the
streets of Dublin, all of which take place between the hours of 3:00 and
4:00 P.M. on Thursday, June 16, 1904. These sections are related only
loosely in terms of narrative and theme, though nearly every section has
at least one element—an object, an image, a gesture—that intersects with
the time and space of at least one other section.

In the tenth section, for example, Bloom stops at a bookseller's cart on
the south bank of the Liffey to buy a book for his wife. Browsing among
the selections of soft pornography, Bloom creates his own private space of
enjoyment beside the continuous flow of traffic (U 10.584f.). At this moment on the opposite bank an elderly female leaves the Palace of the Four
Courts, having heard a "case in lunacy" that, to judge by its full title, is as
convoluted as the infamous suit of Jarndyce and Jarndyce in Dickens's

Bleak House. The woman's appearance serves as a link between this section and the previous one, where, as Lenehan and McCoy approach the spot where Bloom is standing, lawyers at the Four Courts hear rustling from one court to another the same elderly female "with false teeth smiling incredulously and a black silk skirt of great amplitude" (*U* 10.473–75).

The primary and perhaps only purpose of creating this rather aleatory link between one scene and the other is to recreate in textual form the form of city life itself. Of the various formal elements of urban space, the most important for Joyce is that of *circulation*, the constant movement of persons and objects in all directions within a defined space. The importance of circulation to Joyce, both as a formal concept and as a concrete phenomenon, belongs to his concern for addressing the specific conditions of modernity. Foucault makes the point that circulation is one of the defining characteristics of the modern *site*, which has superseded the stable, hierarchized, and sanctified notion of *place* belonging to the Middle Ages. The site is defined by structural relations as in a grid or network and includes "the circulation of discrete elements with a random output" such as automobile or pedestrian traffic (1986, 23). The circulation of capital that forms the economic basis of the city has its physical extension in the circulation of life and machines through the city streets. Machinery, in fact, provides a metaphor for the "Wandering Rocks" chapter, whose nineteen sections can be viewed as interlocking cogs or gears in the great machine of the city. Michel de Certeau has remarked that the city is "simultaneously the machinery and the hero of modernity" (95), meaning that the city generates the historical conditions of modernity while it also becomes a mythic construct in the discourse of modernity. One could say, similarly, that the city is both the machinery and the hero of *Ulysses*. The dynamic of the city drives the narrative of Joyce's work, while it also becomes the principal subject of that narrative.

The final section of chapter 10, which follows the course of the viceregal cavalcade, brings together characters from each of the preceding scenes and organizes them as a series of subjects encountered on a passage through the city, now seen as one great colonial space. At different moments throughout the chapter we have been told of the cavalcade's progress through the city. The lord lieutenant of Ireland and his retinue depart from the viceregal lodge in Phoenix Park, pass through Parkgate and along the northern bank of the Liffey, cross the river at Grattan Bridge, proceed down Dame Street, and eventually cross the Grand Canal into Pembroke Township, where the viceroy is to attend the opening of a charity bazaar for Mercer's Hospital. Along this route, which spans the entire breadth of the city from west to east, the cavalcade passes all the major monuments and institutions that symbolize British rule in Ireland, including the Wellington Monument in Phoenix Park, the Palace of the Four Courts, the police and military headquarters of Dublin Castle, the Bank of Ireland, Trinity College, and the prosperous, mainly Protestant suburb of Pembroke Township. In its itinerary as well as its personnel, this is an imperial tour of a colonial capital, intersecting at various points the routes taken by Queen Victoria on her visits to Dublin in 1849 and 1900.

Despite its machinelike components, the idea of the city as a site of circulating elements can be compared to its textual nature. In this chapter and in *Ulysses* as a whole, the city is treated as a giant text whose elements are buildings, monuments, streets, posters, and shop windows as well as pedestrians and vehicles. Each of these objects constitutes a signifier in a vast network of signification, the reading of which is open to the leisurely observations of someone like Bloom, who has much in common with Baudelaire's *flâneur*, both "perfect idler" and "passionate observer" deriving his enjoyment from "his dwelling in the throng, in the ebb and flow, the bustle, the fleeting and the infinite" (1981, 399). In contrast to the relatively open field of signs implied by this model, the narrative device of the cavalcade transforms the representation of the city into linear time and space. In doing so, it organizes point of view in two ways. On one hand, it produces the commanding and mobile point of view taken from the cavalcade itself, in which the persons and places of the city are seen as a series of objects passed in review. This is literally the imperial point of view, moving across a colonized space with speed and freedom, reading that space as a triumphant manifestation of order and popular good will. On the other hand, the differing points of view of the spectators form an index to the various, complex, and unpredictable responses to the authority of the British Empire—responses that run the entire gamut from the obsequiousness of saluting policemen to the blithe indifference of an unnamed pedestrian in a brown macintosh.

Joyce especially likes to exploit the ironies of unnoticed and misinterpreted gestures of loyalty toward the personages of the cavalcade. At Bloody Bridge, whose name recalls the killing of four Dublin citizens by royal military forces in 1670, the commercial traveler Thomas Kernan greets the viceroy "vainly from afar" (*U* 10.1184). From its sluice in the wall of Wood quay, a conduit known as Poddle River "hung out in fealty a tongue of liquid sewage," showing that in Joyce even inanimate objects have a capacity for irony. Not every gesture read as fealty is so intended:

> On Ormond quay Mr Simon Dedalus, steering his way from the greenhouse for the subsheriff's office, stood still in midstreet and brought his hat low. His Excellency graciously returned Mr Dedalus' greeting. (*U* 10.1199–1202)

No one familiar with the character of Simon Dedalus would interpret his gesture as the greeting of a loyal subject. The irony of this passage depends on the word "greenhouse," slang for a public urinal. Dedalus has just stepped away from this fixture and, having neglected to button his fly, he modestly covers himself with his hat. This is the act received so graciously by the viceroy.

At the tearoom of the Dublin Baking Company in Dame Street, "Buck Mulligan gaily, and Haines gravely, gazed down at the viceregal equipage," while John Howard Parnell looks intently at his chessboard, ignoring the excitement. These three figures form a familiar triad of colonial attitudes. The prosperous Mulligan, whom Stephen Dedalus regards as Ireland's "gay betrayer," speaks condescendingly of his fellow "islanders" (*U* 1.393). Haines, his English guest, observes the passing of the cavalcade with the gravity of one conscious of the burden of conquest. J. H. Parnell, brother of the late Charles Stewart Parnell—the revered leader of Ireland's Home Rule movement—fixes his downward stare in silent protest to the passing scene. Together, the three characters in the tearoom form allegorical figures of the three great forces of Irish history: conquest, resistance, and betrayal.

To these traditional responses to British rule the course of the cavalcade adds more misconstrued and misdirected signs of loyalty. In Joyce's time there stood in College Green opposite Trinity College a frequently vandalized (now destroyed) equestrian statue of William III, whose reconquest of Ireland in 1690 solidified British and Protestant domination for centuries to come:

> Where the foreleg of King Billy's horse pawed the air Mrs Breen plucked her hastening husband back from under the hoofs of the outriders. She shouted in his ear the tidings. Understanding, he shifted his tomes to his left breast and saluted the second carriage. The honourable Gerald Ward A.D.C., agreeably surprised, made haste to reply. (*U* 208)

Hearing the news of the viceroy's passing, Breen mistakenly salutes the wrong carriage, whose passenger, a mere aide-de-camp, is flattered by this unexpected tribute. In one respect the demented Denis Breen, enraged by

imagined insults, serves as a figure for Ireland here as he wanders help-
lessly under the menacing hoofs of British rule. In another, his tardy and
misdirected salute suggests the inherent misunderstandings on which colonial rule is based. In terms of the relations between colonizer and colonized, this scene is structurally equivalent to the one where Simon
Dedalus "brought his hat low." It is characteristic of the history of colonialism that colonial authority suffers from paranoia and overconfidence
at the same time; it sees conspiracies everywhere, while it is eager to con-
strue even ambiguous or misguided gestures of loyalty as evidence of an
entirely natural veneration on the part of its subjects.

In the final lines of the chapter, the cavalcade crosses into Pembroke
Township, where the viceroy is saluted by

> two small schoolboys at the garden gate of the house said to have
> been admired by the late queen when visiting the Irish capital with
> her husband, the prince consort, in 1849. (U 10.1279–81)

Joyce recalls this visit in his Trieste lecture, including the way the Irish
mocked the queen's consort by "greeting him exuberantly with a cabbage
stalk just at the moment when he set foot on Irish soil" (CW 164). He
compares this visit to the queen's only other one, in the spring of 1900,
made during the Boer War, as Joyce ironically observes, "for the purpose of
capturing the easy-going sympathies of the country, and adding to the lists
of the recruiting sergeants" (CW 165). On that occasion the people of the
Irish capital saw "a tiny lady, almost a dwarf, tossed and jolted by the
movements of the carriage, dressed in mourning, and wearing horn-
rimmed glasses on a livid and empty face." Joyce continues,

> [T]he crowd of citizens looked at the ostentatious procession and the
> pathetic central figure with curious eyes and almost with pity; and
> when the carriage passed, they followed it with ambiguous glances.
> (CW 165)

In his historical account of the queen's procession as well as his fictional
account of the viceroy's, Joyce is acutely conscious of the ambiguous nature of imperial authority and of the ways in which power is exercised in
unexpected ways. In the story of the queen's procession, the power of the
gaze resides dramatically with the colonial subjects of Dublin, to whom
their mighty sovereign is revealed as a pathetic and pitiful old woman. In
Ulysses, although the members of the viceregal cavalcade enjoy a com-

manding view during their swift passage through the city, the power of the gaze belongs equally to their colonial subjects, who view them with reverence, insolence, or indifference, as the case may be. Both accounts have the effect of disrupting conventional and unitary notions of power.

Before pursuing this theme further, I wish to go back to a point in the progress of the cavalcade where, as it approaches Pembroke Township along Lower Mount Street, "a pedestrian in a brown macintosh, eating dry bread, passed swiftly and unscathed across the viceroy's path" (*U* 10.1271–72). The identity of this person is much disputed both by Joyce scholars and by characters in *Ulysses*, who have seen him at Patrick Dignam's funeral earlier in the day. For me, however, it is instructive to think of the mysterious man in the brown macintosh as none other than Joyce himself. An hour earlier at the National Library, Stephen Dedalus has argued that Shakespeare has drawn a figure of himself into his own work:

> He has hidden his own name, a fair name, William, in the plays, a super here, a clown there, as a painter of old Italy sets his face in a dark corner of his canvas. (*U* 9.921–23)

With the example of Shakespeare, Joyce alerts us to the presence of his own "signature character" in *Ulysses* that, significantly, appears as a figure both of internal exile from Ireland and of skillful evasion of the effects of colonial rule. Joyce liked to consider himself a Dantean exile and told his students in Trieste that Dante was his "spiritual food" (Ellmann 218). The meal of "dry bread" eaten by the man in the brown macintosh recalls the famous prediction of Dante's exile by the soul of his ancestor Cacciaguida in canto 27 of the *Paradiso*:

> Tu proverai sì come sa di sale
> lo pane altrui, e come è duro calle
> lo scendere e 'l salir per l'altrui scale
> (58–60)[4]

> Thou shalt prove how salt is the taste of another man's bread and how hard is the way up and down another man's stairs. (244–45)

The pedestrian's movement "swiftly and unscathed across the viceroy's path" also recalls, in *Portrait*, the "silence, exile, and cunning" that Stephen must cultivate in order to free himself from the political and historical conditions that trap the souls of the Irish (*P* 269).

Joyce thus portrays himself at the end of the "Wandering Rocks" chapter as a lonely Dantean figure, exiled in his own country, eluding the reach of political power in pursuit of his destiny as an artist. It is important to note, however, that in passing unscathed across the path of power Joyce does not seek refuge in a rarefied aestheticism. On the contrary, it is only his determination, like Dante's, to refuse political affiliation in favor of a "party unto thyself" (*Paradiso* 27.69) that allows him the freedom of a profoundly political analysis of Irish life. In an essay on the Irish poet James Clarence Mangan, Joyce contrasts Mangan's justification of "narrow and hysterical nationality" to the intense life of a poet like Blake or Dante, "taking into its centre the life that surrounds it and flinging it abroad again amid planetary music" (*CW* 82). The theory is that there is a kind of writing so deeply engaged in historical reality that it escapes being enclosed by history. Such is Joyce's own.

The final section of "Wandering Rocks" constitutes Joyce's analysis of the various and contradictory effects of colonial power, as it is fragmented and refracted by a series of complex relations and subjectivities. The political situation as Joyce writes of it cannot be adequately understood by the simple distinction between colonizer and colonized. Nor should modern colonialism in general be seen as a uniform system of repression from the top down but rather as what Foucault calls "a field of force relations, wherein far-reaching, but never completely stable, effects of domination are produced" (1980b, 102). Foucault makes the point that modern institutions of power are not *primarily* repressive or destructive of life; rather they are productive of a certain order of life, and thus they are devoted to "the harnessing, intensification, and distribution of forces, the adjustment and economy of energies" (1980b, 145) as well as, one might add, to the suppression of subversive or insurrectional movements. The purpose of the viceregal cavalcade may be one of imperial ostentation, but its destination is the Mirus bazaar organized to benefit Mercer's Hospital, a charitable institution whose incorporation by Parliament in 1734 serves as an early instance of what Foucault calls "bio-power," wherein "the old power of death that symbolized sovereign power was now carefully supplanted by the administration of bodies and the calculated management of life" (1980b, 139–40). Like Foucault, Joyce reminds us that the regulation of life by modern institutions of power—even the British imperial government in Ireland—fosters support and protection for life as well as repression.

Joyce is neither apolitical nor is he a political writer in the narrowly nationalist sense. Rather, Joyce is a political writer in the sense that every great writer is: he understands the complexities of power at several levels of human relations, including that of the banal activities of everyday life. He demonstrates that there are forms of power other than those exercised by the state and its allied institutions. Finally, his work is testimony to the quite objective fact that the most enduring power is the creative power of the artist.

2

The Comedy of Intolerance
in Proust and Joyce

Given the history of intolerance in twentieth-century Europe, it is significant that two of its most important writers should have been drawn to the scene of anti-Semitism as the particular form of intolerance most worthy of their attention. At a time when other modern writers were still using the stock image of the Jew as an object of ridicule or, conversely, as a noble but accursed wanderer, Proust and Joyce concentrated their satirical force on the discourses and practices that exploited such images. Neither writer, however, was content merely to moralize. Rather, each of them finds a wealth of comic material in the contradictions and the paranoia of anti-Semitism, without submitting to the temptation to ennoble the Jew as victim. In Proust and Joyce, Jews and anti-Semites alike are players in a black comedy where intolerance is rendered both frightening and ridiculous.

Each writer takes up this subject in the context of a specific historical moment. Proust's view is retrospective. Writing during the period from 1912–22, he sets the main part of his story in the 1890s, the era of the Dreyfus affair. While the affair itself remains in the background, Proust focuses on the anti-Semitism of an aristocracy very much oriented toward the past and of diminishing relevance to the political and social realities of the emerging Third Republic. The comedy of this aristocratic intolerance derives from its hypocrisy and its lack of conviction, qualities that seem to reflect an unstated awareness on the part of the aristocracy itself of its anachronistic position in modern France. Their anti-Semitism thus constitutes a sort of rear-guard action on the part of a social class that is already in retreat.

Joyce, in Zürich and then in Paris, wrote *Ulysses* during roughly the same years (1914–22) that Proust was writing *A la recherche du temps perdu*. Where Proust is retrospective, the spirit of Joyce's work is anticipatory. Though set in Dublin in 1904, his novel sets the stage for the coming violence in the struggle for Home Rule, including the Easter Rising of 1914, the ensuing civil war, and the partition of Ireland in 1921. Among the many forms of intolerance marking this era, Joyce concentrates his most explosive episode not on the enmity between Irish and British or that between Catholic and Protestant but on the anti-Semitism of the Irish nationalist movement, whose methods are those of violent provocation. In this early manifestation of fascism, Joyce exposes the contradictions of an ideology that identifies "the Jew" as the source of endemic social conflicts in which Jews historically have no part.

The novelistic episodes that I shall discuss center on scenes of exclusion, or more precisely the expulsion, of Jewish characters from social milieus into which they had been provisionally accepted. In the case of both writers, however, the moral indignation that these stories might otherwise inspire is undermined by a measure of ambiguity and comic equivocation. This apparent avoidance of a consistently articulated ethical position has traditionally been a problem for critics of both Proust and Joyce. Bernard Brun, for example, is among those who point out that Proust's work itself reveals elements of anti-Semitism "dont la valeur n'est rien moins qu'ironique, et il manque au lecteur un point de référence précis qui pourrait le sécuriser" (111) [whose value is not at all ironic, and the reader lacks a precise point of reference that could reassure him]. Brun's solution to this problem is biographical: Proust, himself Jewish on his mother's side and homosexual as well, appropriates the discourse of anti-Semitism in a "masochistic" work that reflects the personal problems arising from family conflict and sexual guilt (128). Similar biographical studies have been written to explain the ambiguity of Joyce's positions.

My own approach, however, is to leave aside speculation on the psychological origins of the work and to treat the work of art as such; that is, I consider ideology as one of the features of language available to the writer for effects of irony, shock, and so on. Julia Kristeva finds, especially in Proust's fictional treatment of Jews and homosexuals, a "sarcastic overloading of discursive codes" from which his characters emerge "ambiguous and unseizable, like the 'transvertebration' of an image in a kinetoscope" (190). Proust and Joyce are notoriously resistant to being reduced to the comfortable logic of the *bien-pensant* and, as writers, they are capable of cruelty as well as compassion. What each of them abhors is ideology itself: its banality, its slavery to the habitual, its intolerance of laughter, of the exceptional, of the unexpected moment of illumination.

In the first part of *Le côté de Guermantes,* Proust describes a matinée at the home of Mme de Villeparisis, a lady of lofty origins who has since fallen in the social order for reasons that the narrator attributes to the nature of her intelligence, "une intelligence presque d'écrivain de seconde ordre bien plus que de femme du monde" (2.482) [an intelligence resembling rather that of a writer of the second rank than that of a woman of position (2.188)].[1] Among her guests is the young Bloch, himself a writer of the second order and one of Proust's great comic characters. As a comical Jew, Bloch is the antithesis of the revered Swann, who belongs to the type of the superior Jew notably manifested in George Eliot's *Daniel Deronda* (1876). Like his fictional antecedent, Swann is alone only because he is more intelligent, more sensitive, and more refined than those around him. As Jeanne Bem remarks, he is "le juif non marqué comme juif" [the Jew not marked as a Jew], and if Swann is "trop peu juif" [not Jewish enough], Bloch is by contrast "trop juif" (103) [too Jewish]. It is precisely this excess that renders Bloch interesting to the society of the Faubourg Saint-Germain. The narrator explains that although the shock waves of the Dreyfus affair were about to cast the Jews down to the bottom rung of the social ladder, those who were unassimilated to the society of the Faubourg were nonetheless the object of an Orientalist taste, so that someone like Bloch remained, "pour un amateur d'exotisme, aussi étrange et savoureux à regarder, malgré son costume européen, qu'un Juif de Decamps" (2.488) [for a lover of the exotic as strange and savoury a spectacle, in spite of his European costume, as a Jew in a painting by (the Orientalist artist Alexandre Gabriel) Decamps (2.194)]. Bloch is, moreover, famous for his gaffes. Having placed his hat on the carpet next to where he is seated in Mme Villeparisis' salon, he warns those entering the room: "Qu'on fasse attention à mon chapeau haute forme" (2.489) [Take care of my top hat (2.196)]. Moments later he overturns a vase of flowers, breaking the glass and spilling water onto the carpet. Adding gaucherie to *maladresse,* he says, "Cela ne présente aucune importance . . . car je ne suis pas mouillé" (2.513) [It's not of the slightest importance; I'm not wet (2.221)].

In spite of his gaucherie, the hostess invites Bloch to seek inside information on the Dreyfus affair from M. de Norpois, a famous diplomat who is also in attendance. Now it happens that Bloch is a passionate Dreyfusard who follows every aspect of the affair, including its repercussions in the trial of Zola, which he attends from morning to night as a member of the public, provisioned with sandwiches and a bottle of coffee. Among the other guests at the home of Mme de Villeparisis, however, there is little sympathy for such convictions. The duc de Guermantes, for example, on hearing that his nephew Saint-Loup is a supporter of Dreyfus, cannot restrain his indignation:

> personellement vous savez que je n'ai aucun préjugé de races, je trouve que ce n'est pas de notre époque et j'ai la prétention de marcher avec mon temps, mais enfin, que diable! Quand on s'appelle le marquis de Saint-Loup on n'est pas dreyfusard, que voulez-vous que je vous dise! (2.532)

> [personally, you know that I have no racial prejudice, all that sort of thing seems to me out of date, and I do claim to move with the times; but damn it all, when one goes by the name of "Marquis de Saint-Loup" one isn't a Dreyfusard. I'm sorry, but there it is.] (2.242)

As Proust points out, there is an ironic discrepancy between the content and the form of this declaration, between the statement of class solidarity with the nobility and the petit bourgeois character of a formula like "quand on s'appelle le marquis de Saint-Loup" [when one goes by the name of "Marquis de Saint-Loup"]. Noblemen like M. de Guermantes are betrayed by the very mediocrity of their expression, which is precisely what discredits Dreyfus himself in the eyes of the duchesse de Guermantes:

> Quelles lettres idiotes, emphatiques, il écrit de son île! Je ne sais pas si M. Esterhazy vaut mieux que lui, mais il a un autre chic dans sa façon de tourner les phrases, une autre couleur. (2.536)

> [What idiotic, turgid letters he writes from his island! I don't know whether M. Esterhazy is any better, but at least he has more of a knack of phrase-making, a different tone altogether.] (2.246)

If one is not against Dreyfus out of class solidarity, one must be so out of literary sensibility.

In his quest for a sympathetic interlocutor, the poor Bloch turns to the young duc de Châtellerault to ask him if it is not true that in other countries people support Dreyfus. Châtellerault, sensing a general disapproval of Bloch among those present, replies, "Excusez-moi, Monsieur, de ne pas discuter de Dreyfus avec vous, mais c'est une affaire dont j'ai pour principe de ne parler qu'entre Japhétiques"[2] (2.544) [Forgive me, Monsieur, if I don't discuss the Dreyfus case with you; it is a subject which, on principle,

I never mention except among Japhetics (that is, Gentiles) (2.255)]. This reply combines cowardice with sadism, but it articulates a basic principle of intolerance: the exclusion from the discussion of those who are its object. This practice has the desired effect of suppressing inquiry, for inquiry is the enemy of exclusion.

There is a Jewish joke about a Jew who is being beaten by a fascist. When the Jew asks why, the beating continues only more fiercely. Again the Jew asks, "Why are you beating me?" to which his persecutor at length replies, "Because you are asking why." Now the society of the Faubourg is not fascist, but its anti-Semitism has in common with fascism a contempt for the spirit of rational inquiry. In their various ways, Mme de Guermantes, her husband, and the duc de Châtellerault are all tacitly acknowledging the superfluity of reason in the persecution of Dreyfus. One does not need reasons to be against Dreyfus or to be anti-Semitic. It may be said of intolerance in general that, like the heart, it has its reasons that reason does not know.

As for M. de Norpois, he soon loses patience in the face of Bloch's interrogation. He retaliates by calling into question the patriotism of Bloch. Once the government has undertaken a revision of the trial, he demands, will Bloch and his fellow Dreyfusards do their duty by respecting whatever measures the government might take? "A son patriotique appel saurez-vous ne pas rester sourds et répondre: 'Présent!'?" (2.542) [When its patriotic appeal sounds, will you have the wisdom not to turn a deaf ear but to answer, "Present"? (2.253)]. Trust in the government's handling of the case is thus rendered a patriotic duty, the equivalent of answering a call to arms against a foreign invasion. M. de Norpois makes the familiar move of questioning the national loyalty of the Jew. Later, M. de Charlus will casually refer to Bloch as a foreigner, to which the narrator, innocently thinking to correct him, will respond that Bloch is French. "'Ah!' dit M. de Charlus, 'j'avais cru qu'il était juif'" (2.584) ["Indeed," said M. de Charlus, "I took him to be a Jew" (2.297)].

If Bloch's fellow guests at the matinée display a contempt for the spirit of inquiry, Bloch himself is made ridiculous by placing too much faith in the search for a truth of the Dreyfus affair. Like the vulgar public, he naively believes in the existence of a "secret dossier," known to the inner circles of government, in which the mysteries of the affair are solved. But Proust reminds us that political truth is rarely so simple, that even a fairly straightforward event such as the confession of Colonel Henry and his subsequent suicide in August 1898 was subject to radically divergent interpretations according to one's political point of view (in the French, 2.538–39; in the English, 2.249). The belief in a secret dossier belongs to the logic of paranoia common to conspiracy theories, themselves a standard element of anti-Semitic mythology, as in the case of the so-called *Protocols of the Elders of Zion*, published in France in 1925, another "secret dossier" that never existed. It is ironic that Bloch, the victim of anti-Semitism, has a view of the world that is as simplistic, if not as malevolent, as the view of those who believe in a conspiracy of Jews. What Proust satirizes in both cases is the mediocre mind and the banality of received ideas.

Bloch is made ridiculous in other ways as well. When de Châtellerault alludes to his Jewish origins, Bloch is astonished that this "secret" has been discovered and reacts in an undignified manner. He blurts out, "Mais comment avez-vous pu savoir? qui vous a dit?" (2.544) [But how on earth did you know? Who told you?], as though, remarks the narrator, he had been the son of a convict (2.255). But how do we evaluate the tone of the narrator here, as he adds, "D'autre part, étant donné son nom, qui ne passe pas précisément pour chrétien, et son visage, son étonnement montrait quelque naïveté" (2.544) [Whereas, given his name, which had not exactly a Christian sound, and his face, his surprise argued a certain naivety (2.255)]. Proust's narrator here demonstrates an ironic disengagement from the character of Bloch that is not wholly consistent with an attitude of sympathy for the victim of anti-Semitism.

Meanwhile, Mme de Villeparisis has been warned by the archivist Gribelin that Bloch may be a spy of the Syndicate, the group of powerful Jewish interests supposed to be behind Dreyfus. When Bloch prepares to take his leave, she wishes to let him know—and to let others know that she is letting him know—that he is not to return. Her manner of expressing herself, however, is a bit like that of the opossum, the North American marsupial that simply feigns death when confronted with a predator. Thus when Bloch approaches her in her large armchair, she appears overcome by a sudden drowsiness and fails to respond to his adieus. The beauty as well as the problem in this method of expulsion is its subtlety, so different from that of "le doigt levé et les yeux flambants" (2.543) [the raised finger and blazing eyes (2.256)] that people imagine. Here the burden of interpreting his fate falls entirely on the guilty one, who must be sufficiently instructed to be able to read the signs of his own banishment. But if he were so instructed, he would be unlikely to have given offence in the first place. So it is no surprise that the deception of Mme de Villeparisis works only too well. Bloch, ignorant of the manner in which a grande dame puts someone out at the door, believes her to be asleep, and raises his voice:

—Adieu, Madame, cria-t-il.
La marquise fit le léger mouvement de lèvres d'une mourante qui voudrait ouvrir la bouche, mais dont le regard ne reconnaît plus. (2.545)

["Good-bye, Madame," shouted Bloch.
The old lady made the slight movement with her lips of a dying woman who wants to open her mouth but whose eyes betray no hint of recognition.] (2.256)

Bloch finally gives up and leaves, thinking that his hostess must be "soft" in the head.

As an act of expulsion, the scene made by Mme de Villeparisis is not very effective. Bloch is the only one who does not know he has been snubbed, and a few days later he is back at the same house. Mme de Villeparisis receives him this time because she is not really unkind, because the archivist is not there to intimidate her, and because a repeat performance would be superfluous, the first having been played to the general appreciation of her acquaintances in the Faubourg.

What then, does one make of this episode as a scene of intolerance? It is paradoxical that in its anti-Semitic form, intolerance in Proust's characters is not simply or even primarily motivated by hatred of Jews but rather by the kinds of vanity exposed in a comedy by Molière. With his commonplace ideas of his own rank, the duc de Guermantes imposes a definite limit to the opinions one can permit oneself to hold "quand on s'appelle" [when one goes by the name of] the duc de Guermantes. The duchesse de Guermantes wishes to uphold her reputation as a wit. The duc de Châtellerault is a coward; the archivist Gribelin a hysteric who predicts a "social war." Charlus is driven by sexual interest in Bloch: his anti-Semitic remarks are designed to camouflage his homosexual desire. As for M. de Norpois, the narrator suggests that his political knowledge is limited to matters of procedure, making him incapable of comprehending anything more profound. Finally, Mme de Villeparisis is motivated by the hope that by skillfully playing the role of a grande dame she will actually achieve that status in the eyes of her audience. Her motives are comparable to those of an entire segment of society, the minor nobility, which seeks to improve its standing by aligning itself against the Jewish colonel. For Charlus, this is the most serious consequence of the affair:

—Tout cette affaire Dreyfus . . . n'a qu'un inconvénient: c'est qu'elle détruit la société . . . par l'afflux de messieurs et des dames de Chameau, de la Chamellerie, de la Chamellière, enfin de gens inconnus que je trouve même chez mes cousines parce qu'ils font partie de la Patrie Française, antijuive, je ne sais quoi, comme si une opinion politique donnaient droit à une qualification sociale. (2.586)

[All this Dreyfus business . . . has only one drawback. It destroys society . . . by the influx of Mr and Mrs Beasts and Beastlies and Fitz Beastlies, whom I find even in the houses of my own cousins, because they belong to the Patriotic League, the Anti-Jewish League, or some such league, as if a political opinion entitled one to a social qualification.] (2.300)

If Proust's characters are anti-Semitic, theirs is an anti-Semitism that is not based fundamentally on hatred of Jews. One might say that anti-Semitism in general is not exactly what it appears to be, that the notion of "the Jew" that it marks out is a pretext for some other lack, some object of internal antagonism that cannot be acknowledged. Like other forms of intolerance, anti-Semitism is always about something other than the other that it designates.

As for Bloch, how suitable is he as the sympathetic victim of intolerance? It is not just that he has bad manners, but that he is also capable of producing the very discourse that vilifies him. When, in the face of the duc de Châtellerault's rebuff, he betrays a shame in his origins, it recalls a scene from the beach at Balbec, where the narrator overhears a torrent of imprecations against the Jews who have invaded the seaside resort:

On ne peut faire deux pas sans en rencontrer . . . on n'entend que 'Dis donc, Apraham, chai fu Chakop.' On se croirait rue d'Aboukir." (2.97)

[You can't go a yard without meeting them . . . you hear nothing but "I thay, Apraham, I've chust theen Chacop." You would think you were in the Rue d'Aboukir.] (1.793)

The narrator is astonished to discover the source of these remarks: his old friend Bloch. This example of Jewish anti-Semitism engages in a double mimicry: Bloch's mimicry of the Yiddish accent takes place within his own more categorical mimicry of anti-Semitic discourse and suggests that this discourse is always in some sense a mimicry of itself. The proliferation of ironic registers, moreover, reinforces the notion implied above that anti-Semitism is a discourse *à la dérive*, a signifier with only an ostensible signified, set into motion to some unacknowledged purpose: in this case, to cover for Bloch's unease concerning his standing at the fashionable resort of Balbec.

*   *   *

In comparing Joyce's work to Proust's, one cannot speak of "influence," except to say that Proust's impact on the literary scene of his time was such that for a younger writer like Joyce working in Paris during the years following the first World War, it would have been impossible to ignore the publication, by Gaston Gallimard's prestigious *Nouvelle Revue Française*, of one stunning volume after another of Proust's great work. In the face of Proust's rapidly mounting importance on the literary scene, Joyce may have found it necessary to perform gestures of independence, which for him characteristically took the form of parody. Thus in *Ulysses* his hero Leopold Bloom at one point appears as a farcical imitation of Proust's narrator. Preparing for bed, Bloom pares his toenail, then inhales its odor with satisfaction.

Why with satisfaction?

Because the odour inhaled corresponded to other odours inhaled of other ungual fragments, picked up and lacerated by Master Bloom, pupil of Mrs Ellis's juvenile school, patiently each night in the act of brief genuflection and nocturnal prayer and ambitious meditation. (*U* 17.1492–96)

There are also acknowledgments of the older writer to be found in Joyce's later work. *Finnegans Wake* describes a certain Miss Fortune "who the lost time we had the pleasure we have had our little *recherché* with" (*FW* 149.23–24), and a later passage recognizes "prouts" as the "poeta" who discovered writing as a "raiding" of the unconscious (*FW* 482.31–32). Proust is important to a reading of Joyce for my present purpose, however, for the symmetry, the coincidence, and the contemporaneity of the two writers in their respective treatments of intolerance.

The world of *Ulysses* is marked by the opposition between the ruling Protestant class and the masses of mostly poor and uneducated Catholics who are, in large measure, the objects of exclusion and colonial domination. This is a social and political divide dating from the English conquest of Ireland in the twelfth century and intensified by the religious divide that dates from the Reformation. Given this background, it may seem surprising that in *Ulysses* the most spectacular incident of intolerance occurs as an expression of Irish nationalist antipathy toward a relatively unimportant minority in Ireland—the Jews.

Where Proust gives us the antitheses of the "good" and the "bad" Jew in Swann and Bloch, Joyce creates a synthesis of the two in the figure of Leopold Bloom—*l'homme moyen sensuel* of petit bourgeois Dublin, a basically comic character who nonetheless manifests qualities of intelligence and sympathy. Bloom is a native-born Irishman of Hungarian Jewish descent on his father's side who has been baptized in both the Protestant and Catholic faiths. Though he practices none of these religions, he is nonetheless identified as a Jew by his fellow Dubliners. Bloom's ambiguous position as both Irish and outsider represents a strategic choice on Joyce's part. Joyce needs a point of view on contemporary Ireland that is thoroughly Irish yet free of the highly politicized perspective of a Catholic or a Protestant. As a writer, Joyce solved this problem by leaving Ireland in order to write about it from the comparatively cosmopolitan perspectives of Trieste, Zürich, and Paris. In *Ulysses*, however, this position of being both inside and outside, Irish and not-Irish, is occupied by Bloom.

Bloom's fateful encounter with the spirit of intolerance occurs in chapter 12 of *Ulysses*, known as the "Cyclops" episode for its parody of the Homeric encounter between Odysseus and Polyphemus. Bloom has gone to a pub called Barney Kiernan's on a mission of mercy: he is looking for the lawyer Martin Cunningham in order to assist the widow of Patrick Dignam, whose funeral he attended earlier in the day. Once there, however, he is confronted by a malevolent character known as the Citizen. Based on a historical personage named Michael Cusack, founder of the Gaelic Athletic Association in 1884, the Citizen is Joyce's parodic figure of a militant Irish nationalism that thrives on myths of cultural and ethnic purity. This formidable character holds forth to the group of regulars at the pub who delight in provoking his xenophobic remarks, partly in sympathy with them, but mainly for their value as a low form of entertainment. The Citizen delivers a litany of imprecations against the familiar objects of nationalist hatred: the British, foreigners in general, the Jews. The latter are "coming over here to Ireland filling the country with bugs . . . Swindling the peasants . . . and the poor of Ireland. We want no more strangers in our house" (*U* 12.1150–51). These remarks are punctuated with the Irish slo-gans of the nationalist party: "*Sinn Fein*! . . . *Sinn Fein amhain*! [Our-selves! Ourselves alone!] The friends we love are by our side and the foes we hate before us" (*U* 12.523–24). The Citizen's wrath against everything foreign extends even to the French, traditional allies of the Irish Catholics in their struggle against the Protestant British:

> The French! says the citizen. Set of dancing masters! Do you know what it is? They were never worth a roasted fart to Ireland. Aren't they trying to make an entente cordial now . . . with perfidious Albion? Firebrands of Europe and they always were. (*U* 12.1385–88)

In this way the 1904 agreement between Britain and France dividing colo-nial North Africa between them and aligning themselves against the Triple Alliance of Germany, Austria-Hungary, and Italy is seen as another be-trayal by France of its coreligionists in Ireland.

In the person of Bloom, however, the Citizen beholds a living and present specimen of a stranger in the house of Ireland:

> —What is your nation if I may ask? says the Citizen.
> —Ireland, says Bloom. I was born here. Ireland.
> The citizen said nothing, only cleared the spit out of his gullet and, gob, he spat a Red Bank oyster out of him right in the corner. (*U* 12.1430–33)

The exchange between Bloom and the Citizen heats up to the point where Bloom is hustled out the door amid anti-Semitic epithets and threats of violence.

Bloom responds with a list of famous Jews (Mendelssohn, Marx, Mercadante, Spinoza), a rhetorical tactic that displays a naiveté worthy of Bloch. In the ideology of atavistic nationalism, nothing is more evident than its conscious and militant anti-intellectualism. To be reminded, there-fore, of Jewish contributions to the history of philosophy and the arts is not to frustrate this ideology but to add fuel to its fire. Bloom's list of famous Jews thus serves as a provocation that is made all the more inflam-matory by the final name on his list: "Christ was a jew like me" (*U* 12:1808–9).

Proust, by the way, would have disputed this point. In a famous passage comparing the "race" of homosexuals to that of the Jews, he notes that the former seek to defend themselves against persecution by recalling that Socrates was a homosexual, just as the latter recall that Christ was a Jew.

The fallacy of this argument, according to Proust, is that there were no "perverts" when homosexuality was the norm, just as there were no anti-Christians before Christ, and that "l'opprobre seul fait le crime" (3.18) [opprobrium alone makes the crime (2.639)]. One can only be a Jew "like Bloom" at a time and place where anti-Semitism exists as the norm. It is not precisely true, then, that Christ, whose crimes were committed against prevailing Jewish law, was a Jew like Bloom, who is not the same kind of Jew, being in a very different position from that of a Jew in the time of Christ. Joyce is aware of this problem in Bloom's reasoning, and this is one of the points at which he measures an ironic distance from his hero.

At the mention of Christ's name, however, the Citizen's wrath turns murderous, in words charged ironically with self-contradiction:

—By Jesus, says he, I'll brain that bloody jewman for using the holy name. By Jesus, I'll crucify him so I will. (*U* 12.1811–12)

Escorted by his friend Cunningham, Bloom escapes down the street, narrowly missed by a biscuit box that the Citizen throws clamorously in his direction.

Putting aside for the moment the violence of this scene in contrast to the studied passivity of the characters at the matinée of Mme de Villeparisis, the Citizen's discourse has many points in common with the anti-Semitism of Proust's characters: the denial of nationality to the Jew, the patriotic appeal, the refusal of dialogue, the recourse to slogans, the tendency to self-mimicry. But beyond the more open hostility depicted in Joyce—a display that corresponds to the social level of his characters—there are important differences between the comic styles of the two writers.

The comic effect of Proust's narrative depends on the ironic distance that separates an essentially sympathetic narrator from a series of characters made ridiculous through their own words and actions. The eccentricities of the narrator himself are compensated for by his apparent sincerity and by the reflective quality of his confessional style, making him a constant and intimate guide to the reader in his explorations of the social universe. Whatever the inconsistencies of Proust's narrative, they are those of a narrative voice made all the more real and present by virtue of those very inconsistencies. The entire project of Proust's work consists in the attempt at establishing the presence and continuity of this personage through the reconstitutive power of memory.

If the fundamental trope of Proust's work is that of recollection, that of

Joyce's is parody: his art depends on the comic possibilities inherent in the nature of language itself. In Joyce everything is subjected to parodic treatment: the convention of a "sincere" and more or less reliable narrator; the enunciation of right-thinking moral principles; even our own attempts, which Joyce has largely anticipated, to occupy a coherent critical position with regard to his work. This supremacy of the parodic mode in Joyce makes for a fictional universe whose ethical implications are, to say the least, extremely complex. Let us look once again, for example, at the passage on nationhood, which begins as Bloom boldly proclaims against "[p]erpetuating national hatred among nations" (*U* 12:1417–18). The statement provokes an interrogation:

—But do you know what a nation means? says John Wyse . . .
—A nation? says Bloom. A nation is the same people living in the same place.
—By God, then, says Ned, laughing, if that's so I'm a nation for I'm living in the same place for the past five years.
—Or also living in different places.
—That covers my case, says Joe. (*U* 12:1419–29)

The attempt to define nationhood degenerates quickly into farce. In this way the attempt to prevent Bloom from claiming Ireland as his nation serves as an occasion for Joyce to question the very idea of nationhood. His treatment of the subject implies that the nation is an ideological fiction that defines itself primarily in negative terms of exclusion. Thus one cannot say precisely what a nation is; one can only say to others, you are not of my nation.

If I am going to call nationhood an ideological fiction, it would be well for me to define what I mean by ideology. Slavoj Žižek defines ideology as a "symbolic solution of real antagonisms," that is, as the imposition of an empty signifier that functions as a container for a variety of mutually exclusive meanings; the same figure is capable of standing for any one of a series of inconsistent contents. Thus in a rare moment of lucidity the Citizen describes the ideology of the British Empire as celebrating the antithetical values of individual liberty and inherited privilege:

The fellows that never will be slaves, with the only hereditary chamber on the face of God's earth. . . . And the tragedy of it is . . . they believe it. The unfortunate yahoos believe it. (*U* 12.1347–53)

If he is capable of analyzing the contradictions in the ideology of British imperialism, the Citizen is also capable of propagating an equally contradictory ideology of Irish nationalism. This ideologically sublime Ireland stands at once for a nation made prosperous through international trade and for an ethnically pure, premodern Ireland, sheltered from the evils of capitalism. The fantasies of this ideology are rendered ironically throughout the "Cyclops" episode by means of a series of parodic interruptions in which the commonplace pub banter is transformed into evocations of Celtic heroes, sentimental descriptions of the Irish landscape, and references to the historical mythology of Ireland as an "island of saints and sages."[3]

The description of the Citizen, for example, casts him in the manner of sentimental nineteenth-century reworkings of Irish legend: "a broadshouldered deepchested stronglimbed frankeyed redhaired freelyfreckled shaggybearded widemouthed largenosed longheaded deepvoiced barekneed brawnyhanded hairylegged ruddyfaced sinewyarmed hero" (*U* 12.152–55). He is one of a long line of such heroes beginning with Cuchulain and Conn of the Hundred Battles and descending (in Joyce's version) to Charlemagne, William Tell, the Last of the Mohicans, the Bride of Lammermoor, and "Patrick W. Shakespeare" (*U* 12:176–91).

Apart from sublime fantasies such as these, Žižek, borrowing an expression from Kant, points out that ideology also has a "negative magnitude," or a symbolic figuration of the evil force that prevents these fantasies from being realised: the Jew is the example *par excellence*. Like the positive fantasies of ideology, however, the contents of this negative magnitude may be multiple and mutually contradictory without weakening the force of the general symbolic structure. In the case of French nationalism, we have noted that Bloch is defined in contradictory ways (foreigner *and* Frenchman lacking patriotism); Bloom is similarly the signifier that performs this negative but multiple function for the proponents of Irish nationalism. The customers in Barney Kiernan's know that Bloom is seeking to assist the widow Dignam, but when he exits briefly to look for the lawyer Cunningham, he is accused of "defrauding widows and orphans" (*U* 12.1622). According to the conflicting stereotypes of the Jew, he is defined alternately as oversexed—"I wonder did he ever put it out of sight" —and sexually emasculated: "Do you call that a man?" (*U* 12.1654). As a Jew, Bloom is grouped with those other invasive foreigners, the British. But on another level of negative magnitude, his racially "debased" origins connect him to the African natives under British colonial domination. Thus, in the increasingly intoxicated mind of the Citizen, Bloom is guilty simultaneously of the brutality of British colonialism and of the savagery of its colonial subjects: "—Is it that whiteeyed kaffir?" (*U* 12.1552).

Since Joyce's critique of ideology is aimed specifically at the level of discourse, the ironic qualities of his narrative show more attention to matters of style than to the more obvious ethical dimensions of his subject. In Joyce, the supremacy of irony extends to the narrative point of view; we are not given the comfort of a morally authoritative voice. Even more so than with Proust, Joyce's reader lacks a secure point of reference from which to observe the scene of intolerance. One notes that the "Cyclops" episode is narrated in the voice of an unnamed, "low" character who speaks the same demotic Dublin English spoken by the regulars at Kiernan's pub. This point of view is drawn from the streets of Dublin; it shares in the fun directed against Bloom, regarding him and the Citizen with about equal measures of irony. To him, the garrulous Bloom, full of layman's versions of scientific theories, is "Mister Knowall" (*U* 12.838), "with his knockmedown cigar putting on swank with his lardy face" (*U* 12.501–2), whereas the enraged Citizen is alternately an amusing spectacle and a public nuisance:

> Arrah, sit down on the parliamentary side of your arse for Christ' sake and don't be making a public exhibition of yourself. Jesus, there's always some bloody clown or other kicking up a bloody murder about bloody nothing. (*U* 12:1792–95)

The narrator's objection to the Citizen, then, is not to his intolerance, but to his disturbance of the peace.

What is often bewildering to students of *Ulysses* is that, in Bloom's dispute with the Citizen, not even his defense of tolerance is spared from parodic disruption. Indignant at the insults he has borne, Bloom declares that he belongs to a race "that is hated and persecuted" and delivers a courageous speech denouncing injustice and hatred:

> —. . . And everybody knows that it's the opposite of that that is really life.
> —What? says Alf.
> —Love, says Bloom. I mean the opposite of hatred. . . .
> —A new apostle to the gentiles, says the citizen. Universal love.

Now there intervenes a new parodic voice, strangely unattributed to any of the characters:

> Love loves to love love. Nurse loves the new chemist. Constable 14A loves Mary Kelly. . . . Li Chi Han lovey up kissy Cha Pu Chow. Jumbo, the elephant, loves Alice, the elephant. . . . You love a certain person.

And this person loves that other person because everybody loves
somebody but God loves everybody. (*U* 12:1493–1501)

It is an innocent and foolish voice, with a child's understanding of love, as
if to demonstrate the hopeless naiveté of Bloom's position. In *A Portrait
of the Artist as a Young Man*, the title character refuses to sign a petition
for "universal brotherhood," apparently regarding it as a threat to his
artistic independence. Here in *Ulysses*, Bloom's eloquent apology for universal love, as well as the slogans of his persecutor, becomes the object of
Joyce's ironizing gestures, as if the writer sensed the danger of subordinat-
ing his art to the well-meaning but well-worn expressions of liberal tolerance.

When, at the end of this encounter, Bloom disappears down the street
pursued by the Citizen's mongrel, his flight is rendered, in a metaphor of
transfiguration, as the ascent of Elijah into heaven:

And they beheld Him even Him, ben Bloom Elijah, amid clouds of
angels ascend to the glory of the brightness at an angle of fortyfive
degrees over Donohue's in Little Green street like a shot off a shovel.
(*U* 12.1915–18)

Joyce's parodic style, his flirtation with delirium, and his mock-heroic gestures combine to rescue the scene of intolerance, as well as the discourse of
tolerance, from the sentimentality of good intentions. The reality of intolerance is made present, but its power is transcended by laughter.

*   *   *

Having rehearsed these scenes from the comedy of intolerance in Proust
and Joyce, we are still left with the question that arises with particular
insistence at the beginning of the twenty-first century: what are the ethical implications of an art that treats both tolerance and intolerance as
comic? For certain readers, the dull earnestness of the question misses the
point of great art. Thus Georges Bataille, writing just after the Second
World War, finds that in Proust, "il ne s'agit plus de changer le monde mais
de le saisir" [it's no longer a question of changing the world but of understanding it], and that "dès lors les spectacles de la vie cessent d'être pour
nous l'objet d'un souci moral" (392) [from now on the spectacles of life
cease to be for us the object of moral concern]. Forty-six years later,
Kristeva holds essentially the same view. Speaking of Proust's narrator, she
writes, "A d'autres de sauver la société si cela leur paraît agréable et pos-

sible. Lui, il ne sauvera qu'un peu de temps à l'état pur, où viendront se ressourcer les déçus de toutes les solutions sociales, forcément vicieuses, forcément criminelles" (201) [It is for others to save society if that appears agreeable and possible to them. As for him, he will save nothing but a little time in its pure state, giving sustenance to the disaffected of all social solutions, which are necessarily perverse, necessarily criminal].

In a similar manner, it is possible to defend Joyce's practice on purely aesthetic grounds by noting that parody is his essential response both to intolerance and to the bourgeois humanistic spirit of tolerance. In Joyce, both of these notions have the status of ironized cultural artifacts, so that we are concerned not so much with an Enlightenment idea of justice as with the form or place of such an idea in the vast network of signs that constitutes the modern world. Joyce's work traces in infinite detail the infrastructure of this network; hence his preoccupation not just with talk but also with the hardware of communications systems, with telephones, gramophones, telegraphs, and cables; with printing presses, billboards, and advertising flyers. As Joyce's work expands to embrace the totality of this system—which is really the system of modern culture itself—the dimensions of the text rival the vertiginous proportions of Borges's "Library of Babel," reputed to contain everything that ever was or could be written in every conceivable language. Derrida has remarked on how Joyce's work constitutes a "machine hypermnésique," a giant computer that seems capable not just of stocking the collective memory of the Western world but also of anticipating every move in the interior world of the modern subject, including the attempt to occupy a critical position external to the Joycean text. For Derrida, nothing transcends the scope of this hyperbolic capacity: "Tout est *intérieur*, téléphonie mentale, tout peut s'intégrer à la domesticité de cette encyclopédie programmotéléphonique" (1987, 100) [Everything is interior, mental telephony, everything can be domesticated by this programmotelephonic encyclopedia]. The universal categories of the Enlightenment begin to lose their distinctive claim here in the limitless chain of signification which Joyce unravels, where any value is susceptible of contamination by whatever value has been traditionally opposed to it.

But is it sufficient simply to defend the aesthetic independence of Proust and Joyce, when both of these writers are so obviously preoccupied with questions of ethical import? A possible solution to the apparent contradiction between aesthetic and ethical concerns is to be found near the end of Proust's own work. In the final volume of *A la recherche du temps perdu*, Proust's narrator is waiting for a piece of music to end before entering the salon of the Princesse de Guermantes, when he experiences a kind of revelation concerning his artistic calling. He realizes that his path as an artist cannot be the one laid out by literary theories developed at the time of the Dreyfus affair then twenty years past, theories designed to make the artist "leave his ivory tower" (3.915) [faire sortir l'artiste de sa tour d'ivoire (4.460)] by calling for an art depicting workers' movements and noble intellectuals—an art devoted, in other words, to the Enlightenment ideals of social justice and the rights of man.

The narrator finds two objections to this notion of art. The first is that "l'art véritable n'a que faire de tant de proclamations et s'accomplit dans le silence" (4.461) [authentic art has no use for proclamations of this kind, it accomplishes its work in silence (3.916)]. Proust makes a familiar distinction between a merely moralizing art and one that establishes its ethical value through its representation of the deeper truths of human nature. Here Proust follows in the tradition of Ruskin, for whom the work of the artist is uniquely that of rendering the object of perception and feeling, not of reason, judgment, or argument (1920, 143).

His second objection, however, is more provocative and, for its time, more original. He finds that the theorists who called for a literature of social justice "employaient des expressions toutes faites qui ressemblaient singulièrement à celles d'imbéciles qu'ils flétrissaient, et peut-être est-ce plutôt à la qualité du langage qu'au genre d'esthétique qu'on peut juger du degré auquel a été porté le travail intellectuel et moral" (4.460) [used hackneyed phrases which had a curious resemblance to those of the idiots whom they denounced. And it is perhaps as much by the quality of language as by the species of aesthetic theory that one may judge the level to which a writer has attained in the moral and intellectual part of his work (3.916)].

Implicitly, Proust is making a claim for the ethical value of an art that pointedly rejects social engagement in favor of its own revolution of the word. Proust's insistence on the quality of language as an essential element of the moral work of the artist is based on the idea of a moral universe constructed in language, but for the artist it is a language that must constantly be recreated in order to avoid the paralysis of "expressions toutes faites" [hackneyed phrases]—a paralysis that, according to this logic, would be moral as well as linguistic. This interpretation of the social value of art recognizes that oppression and intolerance depend ultimately on a certain linguistic construction of reality that is intimately bound up with relations of power. When the intolerant Mr. Deasy declares, "We are a generous people but we must also be just," Stephen replies, "I fear those big words which make us so unhappy" (*U* 2.263–64). The artist's capacity to create a new language—by sabotaging those big words—has a revolutionary potential in the way that it brings into being another way of representing and thus of ordering the world. Intolerance begins as a way of seeing the world according to a set of essentially semantic categories. The comic art of Proust and Joyce is aimed at undermining and destabilizing these categories insofar as they form the ideological foundations of intolerance. It is only through such an art of subversion that a true liberation from intolerance may be imagined as possible.

3

Anthropologies of Modernism

Joyce, Eliot, Lévy-Bruhl

In his 1923 review of *Ulysses*, T. S. Eliot places James Joyce and himself at a moment of convergence with the human sciences that, in his view, has historical consequences for the mission of twentieth-century art:[1]

> Psychology (such as it is, and whether our reaction to it be comic or serious), ethnology, and *The Golden Bough* have concurred to make possible what was impossible only a few years ago. Instead of narrative method, we may now use the mythical method. It is, I seriously believe, a step toward making the modern world possible for art. (1975, 178)

With an oblique reference to his own use in *The Waste Land* of Sir James Frazer's anthropological study, Eliot suggests first of all that new forms of knowledge provide not only material that can be appropriated by art, but also that this knowledge makes possible a completely new artistic form; the newly discovered structures of the unconscious and of "primitive" societies become models for the creation of a new artistic order.

But that is not all, for Eliot goes on to make a claim so ambitious as to carry the conscious risk of not being taken seriously: the artistic method enabled by new knowledge in the human sciences is to be socially regenerative as well as formally innovative. It is a method that has the power of "controlling, of ordering, of giving a shape to the immense panorama of futility and anarchy which is contemporary history" (1975, 177). While Eliot presents Joyce as his ally in this redemptive task, there are reasons to see the author of *Ulysses* as something more like his adversary.[1] Perry Meisel has argued persuasively that Eliot, inspired by his "romance with contemporary anthropology," is in fact propagating a myth of literary history—one "bequeathed to the future as truth"—that precisely opposes the demythologizing strategies of Joyce (87).

Eliot's essay contains the essential elements of this modern myth about myth: that traditional myth, ancient or primitive, stands apart from history; that art as well must escape from history through the repudiation of narrative and the return to its lost origins in myth; that the formal unity achieved in this process alone gives meaning to the contemporary world. Joyce, on the other hand, demystifies the notion of a literary production external to contemporary history; for him, myths and works of art themselves are "overdetermined representations of life" inseparable from history itself (Meisel 7).

While any definition of literary modernism is problematic, one may nonetheless follow Meisel in describing it as writing that sees itself as belated, as coming at the end of history and as thus attempting to originate itself—hence Pound's injunction to "make it new." This self-origination, however, takes the form of a *recovery* of origins in the primitive, in antiquity, in some privileged moment of the past, a retrospective movement that historicizes itself. As Meisel points out, the paradox of modernism is the acknowledged impossibility of its own project: no writing takes place outside history. Paul de Man notes the irony in "defining the modernity of a literary period as the manner in which it discovers the impossibility of being modern" (1983, 144). This impossibility and the irony it evokes become a source of comedy in Joyce; in Eliot it becomes an occasion of despair unless suppressed in the name of a new artistic and cultural order.

The difference between the artistic projects of Eliot and Joyce extends to their respective orientations toward anthropology, which, while being both a science and a purveyor of myths, also has a mythic status of its own. To appropriate a phrase from Derrida, it is a "white mythology" that represents itself as the truth alternately of "man" himself and of the racial or cultural other. Eliot and Joyce both made extensive use of the findings of anthropology, but they differed in the manner and extent to which each accepted the notion of scientific truth offered by the new discipline. Eliot was willing to take it at face value insofar as it contributed to his theories of poetic origins and his attacks on modern civilization. Joyce, however, was acutely conscious of the nature of anthropology as a discursive and mythic *construct* rooted in the colonizing enterprises of European institutions and thought. He satirized the pretensions of anthropology while exploiting its material for his own artistic ends. A particularly suggestive instance of these opposing uses of anthropology is to be found in Eliot's and Joyce's common interest in the French ethnologist Lucien Lévy-Bruhl.

In the following pages I treat each of these three figures in turn. First, I review Lévy-Bruhl's theories of primitive mentality as a controversial development in early modern anthropology.[2] I then discuss the ways in which these theories helped Eliot to formulate a primitivist ideal in his poetry and criticism, one opposed to his pejorative figuration of the Jew. Finally, I explore Joyce's parodies of anthropology and of Lévy-Bruhl in particular, which are both complicated and enriched by questions of knowledge, of Jewishness, and of the nature of writing.

I

Lévy-Bruhl was one of a generation of French intellectuals in the first decade of the twentieth century, including Emile Durkheim and Henri Bergson, who sought to apply philosophical principles to the new sciences of the human mind and society. In doing so he would argue against the rationalist tradition in favor of radically different kinds of knowledge. In an early work on modern French philosophy, he criticizes its reliance on Cartesian method and lucidity in a way that prefigures the modernist sensibility: "Such a philosophy . . . will scarcely admit of the instantaneous divination of the absolute, the mystical intuition which is superior to reason and which dispenses with logical demonstration" (1899, 472).

Under the influence of Durkheim and his most gifted disciple, Marcel Mauss, Lévy-Bruhl moved from traditional philosophical study to ethnology, where he criticized the notion of a universal human nature; instead, he saw a human nature that varied according to differences in civilizations. At the same time, his reading in ancient Chinese philosophy made him question whether non-European cultures might possess modes of thought that were wholly different in kind, and not just degree, from the operations of Western logic (Cazeneuve 2).

This theory of fundamental cognitive difference is central to the two works that made Lévy-Bruhl's reputation: *Les fonctions mentales dans les sociétés inférieures* (1910) and *La mentalité primitive* (1922). In these works Lévy-Bruhl criticizes anthropologists like E. B. Tylor and James Frazer for representing primitive thinking as simply an inferior version of Western logic, as reason misled by ignorance and superstition. Instead, he argues that group ideas or "collective representations" among primitive peoples differ from those of modern civilization in their essentially mystical character. What Lévy-Bruhl calls the "prelogical mentality" follows a "law of participation" that collapses a number of distinctions essential to rational Western thought: between sensible reality and the beyond, or the dream; between present and past or future; between the sign and cause of an event. The phenomenon of multipresence does away with distinctions between one and many, same and other, animate and inanimate: as in the symbolist phenomenon of *dédoublement*, two persons may be distinct from one another and yet the same person; a person may be present in different places at the same time. Time and space are deeply subjective and qualitative and are not subject to Western methods of quantitative measure. The notion of metempsychosis, later to be comically invoked in *Ulysses*,[3] is discovered to be an essential element of the primitive law of participation. The sorcerers of New Guinea, according to Lévy-Bruhl, are believed to have "le pouvoir de métempsychoser les morts dans un serpent, un crocodile, etc." (1922, 42) [the power to metempsychose the dead into a snake, a crocodile, etc.].

Primitive representation itself does away with the distinction between identity and difference:

> [D]ans les représentations collectives de la mentalité primitive, les objets, les êtres, les phénomenes peuvent être, d'une façon incompréhensible pour nous, à la fois eux-mêmes et autre chose qu'eux-mêmes. D'une façon non moins incompréhensible, ils émettent et reçoivent des forces, des vertus, des qualités, des actions mystiques, qui se font sentir hors d'eux, sans cesser d'être où elles sont. (1910, 77)

> [In the collective representations of primitive mentality, objects, beings, and phenomena can be, in a way incomprehensible to us, both themselves and other than themselves. In a way no less incomprehensible, they give forth and receive mystical forces, virtues, qualities and influences which are felt apart from them, without ceasing to remain where they are.]

The primitive mentality, then, does more than represent its object; it becomes part of the object in ways uncanny to the Western mind: "elle le possède et elle en est possédée. . . . Elle en participe au sens non seulement représentatif, mais à la fois physique et mystique, du mot" (1918, 426) [It is possessed by it. . . . It participates in it, not only in the representational sense, but also in the physical and mystical senses of the word].

This mentality was not to be understood as an evolutionary antecedent to Western logic but rather as a completely different mode of thinking free of the law of noncontradiction. The prelogical mentality "ne se complaît pas gratuitement dans le contradictoire . . . mais elle ne songe pas non plus à l'éviter. Elle y est le plus souvent indifférente" (1918, 79) [does not take delight in contradiction . . . but neither does it think of avoiding it. It is most often indifferent to it]. The "mystical intuition" of Lévy-Bruhl's early philosophical work had gone from being reason's superior to reason's cultural other, while it also provided a theoretical basis for interpreting the massive amounts of data gathered by early ethnographers.

James Clifford, who notes Lévy-Bruhl's influence on a generation of modern artists and writers, writes that Lévy-Bruhl's concept of a *mentalité primitive* was among the objects of research that provided fuel for an "ethnographic surrealism" that, unlike the more superficial exoticism of nineteenth-century writers, put reality itself deeply in question (120). André Breton's *Second manifeste du surrealisme* (1930), for example, shares with Lévy-Bruhl the theory of a state of mind unconstrained by logical notions of contradiction:

> Tout porte à croire qu'il existe un certain point de l'esprit d'où la vie et la mort, le réel et l'imaginaire, le passé et le futur, le communicable et l'incommunicable, le haut et le bas cessent d'être perçus contradictoirement. (1973, 76–77)

> [There is every reason to believe that the mind reaches a point at which life and death, real and imaginary, past and future, communicable and incommunicable, high and low, cease to be perceived as contradictory.]

The surrealists were appropriating theories of the primitive, as well as of the unconscious, in their own attempt to create a new order.[4]

By the 1920s, Lévy-Bruhl had become a major figure in ethnological study. In 1925 he founded, with Mauss and Paul Rivet, the Institut d'Ethnologie at the University of Paris, which trained professional scholars, fieldworkers, and colonial officials in the principles of ethnology. Only two years later, however, Lévy-Bruhl resigned from the institute amid differences with his colleagues. Mauss, following Durkheim's example, emphasized the study of human behavior and considered *ritual* the key to understanding primitive or modern societies. But Lévy-Bruhl, always a philosopher in essence, was interested in *myth* and the light it cast on the workings of the human mind (Littleton x). Leaving the university, he nonetheless continued in his influential position as editor of the *Revue philosophique* and wrote four more books on primitive mentality, mythology, and mysticism.

Lévy-Bruhl's resignation coincided with mounting criticism of his theories of primitive mentality. There were two principal objections: one was to Lévy-Bruhl's formulation of "laws" and his composite picture of the primitive mind, which extended even to the natives of India and China. Mauss and Bronislaw Malinowski, among others, were moving toward ideas of the plurality and specificity of cultures. A more forceful objection, not wholly compatible with the first, was to what seemed an unbridgeable chasm that Lévy-Bruhl had drawn between two kinds of human mentality; primitives, after all, were capable of logical thought, while even advanced societies retained elements of the mystical. In *La pensée sauvage* (1962), Claude Lévi-Strauss would eventually argue in a definitive manner against his former teacher's theory that there are fundamentally qualitative differences between modes of thought in different cultures: "contrairement a l'opinion de Lévy-Bruhl, cette pensée [sauvage] procède par les voies de l'entendement, non de l'affectivité; à l'aide de distinctions et d'oppositions, non par confusion et participation" (1962, 355) [contrary to the opinion of Lévy-Bruhl, (primitive) thinking proceeds by way of understanding, not affectivity, with the aid of distinctions and oppositions, not confusion and participation].

Faced with this kind of criticism, Lévy-Bruhl gradually moved toward a position based on the polarity of the two mentalities: both could be found in all societies but in differing proportions. Modern civilization carries with it a "residue" of the mystical and the prelogical (Mercier 115). Indeed Lévy-Bruhl had formulated a version of this theory as early as 1910, where he argued that modern society retains elements of the mystical and prelogical in its religious and political institutions (1918, 455).

In the end, however, much of his theory would not stand up even for Lévy-Bruhl himself; he recanted major parts of it in notebooks published after his death in 1939. There, for example, he abandoned the notion of a prelogical mentality indifferent to contradiction: he now believed that primitives were sensitive to contradiction but simply failed to perceive it when transported to the level of mystical experience. He acknowledged that his earlier work had run the greatest possible risk by postulating an "impossibility of understanding" separating the modern mind from the primitive (1949, 51–60).

Apart from the changing fortunes of Lévy-Bruhl's ideas in the anthropological world, one may recognize in his language some of the fundamental concerns of twentieth-century writing in general, even as it moves into what is called the postmodern era: the conflict between reason and its others; the crisis of representation; the problem of the subject; the questions of power and tradition and their relation to a collective, unconscious order. In any case, the imaginative possibilities inherent in Lévy-Bruhl's theory proved more attractive to the literary avant-garde of the twenties than to many of his fellow anthropologists.

II

Lévy-Bruhl was precisely the kind of wide-ranging, highly provocative continental philosopher to have attracted Eliot's early interests in epistemology, mysticism, and the symbolic formations of non-Western cultures. Where works like *The Golden Bough* were of value to Eliot primarily as sources of mythic material, Lévy-Bruhl provided a theoretical framework for this material that helped Eliot to think through his own ideas on the poetic process and contemporary culture. Eliot himself distinguishes between Frazer's "accumulation and collocation of material" and the "construction of this material into a single edifice" by original thinkers like Durkheim and Lévy-Bruhl (1924b, 489).[5]

Eliot read Lévy-Bruhl in 1913 as a student in Josiah Royce's seminar at Harvard, where he presented a paper on "The Interpretation of Primitive Ritual," comparing Lévy-Bruhl, Durkheim, Frazer, and Jane Harrison.[6] Here Eliot is concerned with the *origin* of primitive ritual and with the fact that no anthropological theory seems adequate to it. He follows Lévy-Bruhl in criticizing the English anthropologists' theory of a "uniform mind" based on modern logic: "Any theory which attributes the genesis of religious thought to the operation of logical reasoning . . . is bound to be unsatisfactory" (quoted in Gray 121). In a second paper delivered in the spring term of 1914, Eliot cites Lévy-Bruhl's law of participation as a kind of unified ground for human understanding, which only later gets separated into "ideal constructs" like cause and volition (G. Smith 138). He insists that there is no essential difference between the *mentalité primitive* and that of contemporary life. Even at this early stage, then, Eliot is engaged in a characteristically modernist project: the search for a mythic origin, the identification of this origin as a repressed element of modern consciousness, and the acknowledgment of the problematic nature of its recovery.

In Eliot's doctoral dissertation on F. H. Bradley, written in England during the next two years, Lévy-Bruhl is cited to demonstrate that abstract ideas common to logical thinking are specifically modern, or "late in the order of knowledge," and are thus different from those of primitive societies (1989, 105). They constitute a level of overlay both historically and within the modern mind itself. At the same time, notions of immediate experience and of "feeling"—both distinct from and prior to logical categories—acquire the same values of an original, timeless, and undifferentiated unity that Eliot finds in Lévy-Bruhl's law of participation: "In feeling the subject and object are one" (21). This notion of feeling will later figure in Eliot's most original essay on the poetic process, "Tradition and the Individual Talent" (1919), where feeling is a kind of raw material, deeper, more essential, more impersonal—more *primitive*—than mere "emotion": "great poetry may be made without the direct use of any emotion whatever: composed of feelings solely" (1975, 41).

The original unity of the *mentalité primitive* may also be compared to the unified sensibility Eliot attributes to the English metaphysical poets. Marc Manganaro (1986, 100) locates in Lévy-Bruhl a source for the theory of "dissociation of sensibility," Eliot's memorable phrase for the symptom from which poetry has suffered since the seventeenth century and from which "we have never recovered" (1975, 64). In *Les fonctions mentales*, Lévy-Bruhl writes that for the primitive mind objects and their mystical properties form an integral, synthetic whole (*un tout indécomposable*). It is only later in the course of social evolution that what we call natural phenomena become the sole object of perception, to the exclusion of elements that are then relegated to the status of superstition. "But as long as this 'dissociation' does not take place, perception remains an undifferentiated unity" (1918, 39). Thus for Eliot the *mentalité primitive* was adaptable to different critical purposes; it could serve as the model both for a component of the individual poetic process and for a privileged moment in literary history.

Eliot confronts Lévy-Bruhl most directly in a 1916 review that comments at some length on *Les fonctions mentales des sociétés inférieures*. Here Eliot is most interested in the case of the Bororo tribesman of Brazil (later studied by Lévi-Strauss) who has a parrot for his totem. The Bororo man has not merely adopted the parrot as a heraldic emblem or mythic figure, nor is he deluded into thinking he is a parrot. Rather, he is capable of a state of mind in which he *is* a parrot, while being at the same time a man. The Western mind, Eliot believes, has lost or suppressed this capacity belonging to the prelogical mind:

> In other words, the mystical mentality, though at a low level, plays a much greater part in the daily life of the savage than in that of the civilised man. M. Lévy-Bruhl goes on to insist quite rightly upon a side of the primitive mind which has been neglected by older anthropologists, such as Frazer, and produces a theory which has much in common with the analyses of mythology recently made by disciples of Freud. (1916, 16)

Eliot may have in mind Jung's *Wandlungen und Symbole der Libido* (1912), which appeared in English translation as *Psychology of the Unconscious* that same year, 1916. In the background lies the work of Freud himself, who in *Totem und Tabu* (1913) had sought to bridge the gap between anthropology and psychoanalysis by finding a residue of "savage" mentality in certain contemporary forms of neurotic obsession. In any case, Lévy-Bruhl's work provides Eliot the occasion to establish an implied analogy between the primitive "mystical" mentality and the unconscious in modern life, both of which would figure in Eliot's work. In his analyses of the creative process, Eliot will insist on the primary role of the unconscious in the production of poetic language, while his cultural criticism will appropriate a primitivist version of mystical consciousness as an essential element of the ideal social order.

One of the consequences of anthropology was that its wealth of descriptive material could simply be appropriated by artists for purposes far removed from the world that formed the original objects of description. Just as primitive artifacts were collected by European museums and incorporated into cubist paintings, verbal images of primitive ritual found their way into modernist writing. This appropriation often took the form of a confrontation or encounter with the primitive. Nineteenth-century exploration narratives, an early source of anthropological data, had dramatized the European encounter with the native other as part of the ideology of imperial expansion. As Edward Said, Christopher Miller, and others have shown, twentieth-century writers from Conrad to Céline continually rewrote this mythic moment as part of an aesthetic project. The encounter with the racial, cultural, or psychological other became an occasion for modernist writers to remythologize both the modern world and their roles within it.

In one version of this modernist appropriation, Eliot saw primitive consciousness as belonging not only to exotic peoples but as a latent power within contemporary life.[7] As if anticipating Lévy-Bruhl, Eliot's early poems often struggle to contain a barely controlled atavism that threatens to shatter the fragile veneer of civilization:

> Inside my brain a dull tom-tom begins
> Absurdly hammering a prelude of its own.
> (1952, 9)

The speaker in "Portrait of a Lady," trapped into complicity with the platitudes of the literary salon, compares his degraded position to that of a performing animal:

> And I must borrow every changing shape
> To find expression . . . dance, dance
> Like a dancing bear
> Cry like a parrot, chatter like an ape
> (1952, 11)

In this figure the metaphor of degradation is accompanied by the liberation of poetic rhythm in a moment of animal mimesis that, like the beating tom-tom, recalls certain forms of primitive ritual; the poem draws on this ritual to effect a kind of emotional release from the stultifying sentimentalities of his hostess.

The Waste Land presents primitive ritual not as an escape but as a lost origin of order and meaning. The formal order of ancient fertility rites and vegetation ceremonies are recovered, if rearranged, in the formal order of the poem itself so as to impose meaning on contemporary history's panorama of futility and anarchy. It does not matter that the meaning imposed is a negative one, that the poet's commanding view is precisely one of disorder; the redemptive power of myth, its order outside history, remains intact. At the same time, the myths of Adonis, Attis, and Osiris borrowed from Frazer join Europe and the Orient in a distant past and so have the value, for a poet in the waning era of imperialism, of uniting Europe with its colonized other in an idealized mythic identity. This appropriation of primitive fertility rites may be compared with Eliot's use of the Buddhist Fire Sermon and the *Brihadaranyaka Upanishad*, both abstracted from their respective cultural contexts and joined with other myths in the universalizing movement of the poem.

Eliot's poetic mastery, however, allows him to play the conventions of primitivist discourse in more than one register. The title character of *Sweeney Agonistes* (written 1923–25), for example, proposes a comic inversion of the mythic colonial encounter in music-hall cadences:

> I'll be the cannibal . . . I'll convert *you*!
> Into a stew.
> A nice little, white little, missionary stew.
> (1952, 80)

Inspired by such images, the song of the Aristophanic chorus parodies a number of conceptions of the primitive. Lévy-Bruhl had written, for example, that in the *mentalité prélogique*, "l'opposition entre l'un et le plusieurs, le même et l'autre, etc., n'impose pas la nécessité d'affirmer l'un des termes si l'on nie l'autre, et réciproquement" (1918, 77) [the opposition between one and many, same and other, etc., does not impose the necessity of affirming one of the terms if the other is denied, and vice versa]. In the version of the *Sweeney* chorus:

> Under the bamboo tree
> Two live as one
> One live as two
> Two live as three
> Under the bam
> Under the boo
> Under the bamboo tree
> (1952, 81)

A subsequent verse offers up the standard romanticization of the primitive, in modern art and culture, as an object of erotic desire, "Where the Gauguin maids / In the banyan shades / Wear palmleaf drapery." Despite these ironic gestures, the controlling metaphor of the play remains the somber one of modern life as a desert island, an unredeemed place of "birth, copulation and death" reduced to a zero-degree level of existence:

> You see this egg
> You see this egg
> Well that's life on a crocodile isle.
> (80)

Eliot's darkest poem, "The Hollow Men" (1925), rewrites in more haunting tones this projection of the modern subject onto the primitive as a space of absence. For an epigraph, Eliot quotes the grotesque line from *Heart of Darkness:* "Mistah Kurtz—he dead." Introduced in this context, the primitive is the insolent harbinger of death represented by the fragmented artifacts of a shabby ritual: "Headpiece filled with straw / . . . Rat's coat, crowskin, crossed staves." In this particular appropriation, the subject's identification with the abject forms of primitive ritual constitute his most damning confession:

> We are the hollow men
> We are the stuffed men
> (1952, 56)[8]

In later years Eliot would return continually to a myth of the primitive, borrowed partly from ethnology, to support his ideas on poetry and culture. In *The Use of Poetry and the Use of Criticism* (1933), for example, Eliot writes that "poetry begins . . . with a savage beating a drum in a jungle," adding that "it may make us from time to time a little more aware of the deeper, unnamed feelings which form the substrata of our being, to which we rarely penetrate" (155). More than a metaphor, the figure of poetry's savage origins acquires scientific authority from ethnological research. Eliot cites an article by two French ethnologists who, having done fieldwork in Madagascar, use the theories of Lévy-Bruhl to compare the structures of the primitive mind to those of the symbolist poem. Emile Cailliet and Jean-Albert Bedé argue that the symbolists achieve the richly intuitive suggestiveness of their language by disrupting the balance between rational and mystical forces that, according to Lévy-Bruhl, belong to highly evolved peoples. The symbolists thus move in a sense back through time, finding a "precivilized" mental state at the depths of their being: "Le symbolisme institue la vaste expérience de la resurrection du primitif" (369) [Symbolism institutes the vast experience of the resurrection of the primitive]. Eliot's comment on this article notes the debt to Lévy-Bruhl and summarizes the argument as follows: "The prelogical mentality persists in civilised man, but becomes available only to or through the poet" (148). The origin of poetry is thus located simultaneously in prehistory, primitive culture, and a primitive consciousness indistinguishable from contemporary notions of the unconscious.

This "reascending to origins" in search of the source of poetry has its counterpart in Eliot's cultural criticism, where so-called primitive societies provide a crude model for his utopian visions. In *The Idea of a Christian Society* (1940), Eliot finds in "the life of the savage . . . the operation of a social-religious-artistic complex which we should emulate upon a higher plane" (1968, 49). In addition to the savage's strong sense of relation to nature and to the supernatural, Eliot admires what he perceives as the highly integrated, organically pure structure of such societies. The implications of this idealization are clear in *After Strange Gods*, the published version of Eliot's 1933 lectures at the University of Virginia. Here Eliot's ideal of a traditional society is based on an organic unity that takes its purest form in blood kinship, rootedness in a single place, and a shared sense of taboo. A consequence of this primitivist ideal is Eliot's infamous remark that "reasons of religion and race combine to make any large number of free-thinking Jews undesirable" (1934, 20). In other words, the Jew must be excluded precisely because he is the ultimate inassimilable element and thus a constant source of instability to what would otherwise be a coherent, unified whole. In what I shall call an ethnomythology, Eliot's discourse puts the respective figures of savage and Jew in polar opposition: the one an undifferentiated, original unity; the other wandering dangerously beyond the outer limit, an object of perpetual exclusion because disruptive of that mythic unity.

Eliot's figure of the Jew typically signals the corruption of a once noble cultural order, represented variously as the Old Dominion of Virginia, early-seventeenth-century England, or Renaissance Italy. A 1915 letter to Eleanor Hinkley compares certain "brilliant" students at Oxford to "the clever Jew undergraduate mind at Harvard; wide but disorderly reading, intense but confused thinking, and utter absence of background and balance and proportion. I should expect it to be accompanied by a philistine aristocracy" (1988, 92). This would not be far off as a description of Eliot's own undergraduate career. For all his family history, Eliot was still the son of a midwestern brick manufacturer who had few friends at Harvard and studied with "an almost willful intensity," according to Peter Ackroyd (33–35). In England, Bertrand Russell snobbishly described Eliot to Lady Ottoline Morrell as an example of well-mannered American "window dressing" (Ackroyd 50), and Lyndall Gordon writes that at Garsington, the Morrells' Oxfordshire estate, Eliot's "ostentatious learning . . . did not impress" (83). The fear of being perceived as a philistine in upper-class English society may partly account for, though it hardly excuses, the malevolent portrayal of Jews in Eliot's early poems.[9]

A fair example is "Burbank with a Baedeker: Bleistein with a Cigar"

(1919). In this poem the once enchanting Venice of Canaletto, Mantegna, and Galuppi has become a place of corruption, personified in the decadent aristocrat Princess Volupine and her adulterous relations with *arriviste* figures like Sir Ferdinand Klein. The abject Bleistein, "Chicago Semite Viennese," both presides over and underlies the scene of Venice's decline:

> The rats are underneath the piles.
> The jew is underneath the lot.
> (1952, 24)

In Eliot's historical vision, this debased figure of the Jew stands "at the smoky candle end of time" in antipodal relation to the savage; history begins with the purity of the primitive and ends, in chaos and futility, with the adulteration of the Jew. Eliot's specific exclusion of "free-thinking" Jews from his ideal cultural order in *After Strange Gods*, however, poses another problem.[10] He would appear to perceive a danger in rational thought itself when it is unrestricted by boundaries of genetic and geographic origin—boundaries not themselves the product of a rational order. "We" are to use our minds to discover what is best for us "as a particular people in a particular place" (1934, 19). Thinking, then, ultimately must be confined by the nonrational, by something outside or prior to reason itself. The perils of *this* reasoning have been parodied in advance, in the "Cyclops" episode of *Ulysses*, where Leopold Bloom defines *nation* as "the same people living in the same place. . . . Or also living in different places," but his thinking is free enough to bring a historical perspective to the immediate occasion, one of Jew-baiting: "And I belong to a race, too . . . that is hated and persecuted. Also now. This very moment. This very instant" (*U* 12.1467–68). Putting Bloom aside for the moment, there is no better examplar of the free-thinking Jew than Lévy-Bruhl himself, a Dreyfusard, a supporter of the socialist Jean Jaurès, a contributor to *L'Humanité*, an activist for the *Front populaire*, an acquaintance of Freud, and a reader of Joyce (Cazeneuve xi–xv; Ellmann 696).

III

It is possible to see in Joyce, as in Eliot, an attraction to Lévy-Bruhl's "primitive consciousness" as a realm of signification that brings together myth and history, dream and reality, conscious and unconscious, present and past, in ways denied by a rationalist, materialist age. In *Ulysses* and especially *Finnegans Wake*, we witness the disappearance of causality, the merging of subject and object, the multiple presences of a single being, the unhinging of time from space, the elaboration of an "unlimited field" of mythic representation that exceeds any counterpart in objective reality.

Unlike Eliot, however, Joyce sees in anthropology as a discipline the tyranny of the rational, colonizing mind intent on objectivizing or romanticizing the lives of subject peoples. He has little patience for nostalgic myths of the primitive of the kind that were being purveyed by W. B. Yeats and Augusta Gregory. Reviewing *Poets and Dreamers*, Augusta Gregory's account of Irish folklore in 1903, Joyce refers to the West of Ireland as "a land almost fabulous in its sorrow and senility." He maintains an ironic distance from anthropological studies of the peasants:

> It is difficult to judge well of their charms and herb-healing, for that is the province of those who are learned in these matters and can compare the customs of countries, and indeed, it is well not to know these magical sciences, for if the wind changes while you are cutting wild camomile you will lose your mind. (*CW* 103)

In *Ulysses*, anthropology's chief representative is the Englishman Haines: patronizing, dull-witted, and anti-Semitic. His projected book on Irish folklore is derided by Mulligan—"five lines of text and ten pages of notes about the folk and the fishgods of Dundrum"—while Stephen sees him as a representative of the "imperial British state."

This is but the first in a series of parodies of ethnographic knowledge scattered throughout the text of *Ulysses*. In the "Lestrygonians" episode, Bloom recites a ribald limerick about a cannibal chief who, upon eating a white missionary, sees his sexual prowess grow to amazing proportions: *His five hundred wives. Had the time of their lives. . . . It grew bigger and bigger and bigger* (*U* 8.778–83). In keeping with this interest in exotic sexuality, the revelers in "Oxen of the Sun" retail a fantastic account concerning the wedding rite of Madagascar for the disrobing and deflowering of spouses. "[S]he to be in guise of white and saffron, her groom in white and grain, with burning of nard and tapers, on a bridebed while clerks sing kyries and the anthem *Ut novetur sexus corporis mysterium* [that the whole mystery of physical sexuality may become known] (*U* 14.345–48).[11] Here a mock hymn is joined with mock ethnography in an ornate latinate style that parodies Sir Thomas Browne's *Pseudodoxia Epidemica* (1646), itself devoted to the "vulgar errors" of popular wisdom concerning

Jews, gypsies, pygmies, Negroes, and other objects of bogus ethnographic knowledge. The effect of Joyce's technique is to turn ethnographic knowledge itself into a kind of folklore, thus dissolving the boundary between the traditional form and the object of knowledge, while satirizing ethnographic knowledge itself as a construct embedded within the discourses of race, religion, sexuality, and imperialism. In Joyce's universe there is not knowledge on one side and its object on the other; instead, there is a proliferation of discourses distinguished from one another by stylistic and rhetorical difference rather than by their epistemological claims to truth.

There is, finally, in the "Eumaeus" episode, the postcard from Bolivia entitled "Choza de Indios." It shows "a group of savage women in striped loincloths, squatted, blinking, suckling, frowning, sleeping amid a swarm of infants (there must have been quite a score of them) outside some primitive shanties of osier" (U 16.475–78). The scene is a visual cliché of the abject primitive, a tired way of seeing that corresponds to the weary, long-winded voice of the narrator. It is left to Murphy, the bibulous sailor, to provide commentary: "Chews coca all day, . . . Stomachs like breadgraters. Cuts off their diddies when they can't bear no more children. See them sitting there stark ballocknaked eating a dead horse's liver raw" (U 16.479–81). Bloom, noting the postcard's lack of message and its partially obliterated, apparently fictitious address, is led to doubt the veracity of the sailor.

These doubts are to my purpose, because the postcard and its owner together represent a debased ethnography, a dubious text presented by an untrustworthy interpreter. If debased, however, its value as interpretation is neither greater nor less than that of the Oxford-educated Haines, whose father, we learn from Mulligan, made his money by "selling jalap [a purgative] to Zulus or some bloody swindle or other" (U 1.156–57). Elsewhere Stephen Dedalus will accuse a personified Erin in biblical tones: "thou didst spurn me for a merchant of jalaps" (U 14.372–73), thus identifying two colonized peoples, the Irish and the Zulus, as victims of the same swindle. Joyce had written in a 1907 essay that "the Englishman has done in Ireland only what the Belgian is doing today in the Congo Free State" (CW 166). In its filial relation to imperialist commercial exploitation, Haines's "respectable" ethnography appears just as banal as a sailor's postcard. Joyce implicitly calls into question the ethical and intellectual value of ethnography per se and sees it as part of a larger colonizing enterprise.

On a visit to Copenhagen in 1936, Joyce met Lévy-Bruhl, who turned out to be an admirer of Ulysses (Ellmann 696), and who presented Joyce

with two of his own books (Connolly 24). Joyce attached enough importance to this particular reader that, three years later, he arranged that
Lévy-Bruhl (and Eliot, who had published parts of *Work in Progress*) be
sent an article on *Finnegans Wake* engineered by Joyce to appear in the
Nouvelle Revue Française (Mercanton 85). Lévy-Bruhl also had reason to
be interested in the *Wake,* for he appears there in parodic form in the guise
of a series of personages named as authorities in an impossibly convoluted
discourse on the nature of time and space.

In the "picture gallery" chapter (*FW* I.6), a certain Professor Jones
(Shaun) is asked, in the cadences of an Irish ballad, if he would come to the
aid of a poor exile in need (Shem):[12]

> If you met on the binge a poor achesyeld from Ailing, when the tune
> of his tremble shook shimmy on shin, while his countrary raged in
> the weak of his wailing, like a rugilant pugilant Lyon O'Lynn ... if the
> fain shinner pegged you to shave his immartial, wee skillmustered
> shoul ... we don't think, Jones, we'd care to this evening, would you?
> (*FW* 148.33–149.10)

The exile from Ireland, like Joyce, is part singer, part Sinn Feiner, and a *fain*
[willing] sinner who nonetheless begs for the salvation of his immortal,
unmartial, schoolmastered, *sheol*-destined soul.

The musically affective quality of this plea contrasts sharply with
Jones's refusal, designed to "confute this begging question" by means of an
abstract, blustering argument against time. Disavowing the need to "an-
thrapologise for any obintentional ... downtrodding of my foes," he cites
his scholarly allies: Professor Loewy-Brueller, author of an account of "the
Sennacherib as distinct from the Shalmanesir sanitational reforms"; Professor Levi-Brullo, F.D. [*Fidei Defensor* (defender of the faith)], who ex-
periments absent-mindedly by holding an egg in one hand while boiling
his watch on the stove; and Professor Llewellys ap Bryllars, F.D., Ph.D.,
who supports Jones's views on the solidity of space as against the immate-
riality of time. The "waste of time" is "what the romantic in rags pines
after ... while, for aught I care for the contrary, the all is *where* in love as
war" (*FW* 151.17–36). In this last incarnation, Lévy-Bruhl merges with
Wyndham Lewis, who in *Time and Western Man* (1927) had attacked
Ulysses for its treatment of time as "einsteinian flux" and had declared, "I
am for the physical world" (130). [The *Wake* will later return to Lewis's
book, retitling it and adding an advertisement: "*Spice and Westend*

Woman (utterly exhausted before publication, indiapepper edition shortly)" (292.6).]

Among the multiple incarnations of Lévy-Bruhl, we find lurking in the background not just Lewis but also the figure of the amateur anthropologist Haines. Loewy-Brueller has given a confessional talk entitled, "Why am I not born like a Gentileman and why I am now so speakable about my own eatables" (*FW* 150.26). The theme recalls Haines's suspicion, revealed in the opening pages of *Ulysses*, that Stephen is not a gentleman. This conforms with Haines's desire to treat Stephen as an authentic source of indigenous folklore and suggests that the relation of the anthropologist to his subject is comparable to the class-based relation of gentleman to peasant. Lewis, incidentally, had diagnosed Joyce as having a "gentleman complex" and called him "the poet of the shabby-genteel" (93), casting essentially the same doubts on Joyce's social position that Haines casts on Stephen.

Joyce's pun on "Gentile," however, complicates matters by raising the issue of Lévy-Bruhl's Jewishness, with a glancing allusion to Giovanni Gentile, the Italian philosopher of fascism who figures in Lewis's book. Indeed the above-mentioned "confession" is given a fantastic bibliographic reference: "Feigenbaumblatt and Father, Judapest, 5688, A.D." (*FW* 150.27). We note, parenthetically, that Bloom's Jewish father had lived in Budapest, and that according to Roland McHugh (*Annotations*) 5688 Anno Mundi is 1927 A.D., the publication date of *Time and Western Man*, in which Lewis said Joyce had "certainly contributed nothing to the literature of the Jew, for which task he is in any case quite unsuited" (118). Instead of contributing to an ethnographic literature of the Jew, however, there is evidence that Joyce thought of literature itself as Jewish in origin, as if the mythical publishing house—its name recalling the first fig-leaf-covered confession to God the Father (Genesis 3)—were the original source of textual dissemination among the Semitic peoples scattered by the destruction of Babel. Writing, in its character as the Fall, as diaspora, thus becomes the condition for ethnography as well as for Joyce's own Babelian text.

In Joyce's mythology the figure of the Jew is often allied with that of the poet; both live in exile, finding their identities not in landed title but through writing, the book, and a privileged relation to spiritual and visionary reality. The poet is again like the Jew in his rarefied dietary regimen, living on the manna of inspiration. Derrida writes, quoting Edmond Jabès:

The Poet and the Jew are not born *here* but *elsewhere.* They wander, separated from their true birth. Autochthons only of speech and writing, of Law. *"Race born of the book"* because sons of the Land to come. (1978, 66)

There is an aspect of anthropology that shares these conditions. The anthropologist is a wanderer among the Gentiles, in the original sense of this word as designating the indigenous, autochthonous, pagan peoples of other lands—the tribes of Shalmenesir and Sennacherib as well as the Bororos. He remains an exile in their midst, for his allegiance is finally to the law of writing and of the book. In this way Lévy-Bruhl, neither Gentile nor "gentleman" in the sense that the anti-Semite Haines would insist on, is allied to Stephen, to Shem the exiled poet, and ultimately to Joyce himself.

Having left the subject with Eliot, I will return briefly to the opposition between the primitive and the Jew within the discourses of ethnomythology, or the traditional mythologies of the other. Like Joyce's writing, the theories of Maurice Blanchot undermine the manner in which this opposition is conceived by a writer like Eliot. In *The Infinite Conversation,* Blanchot writes on Jewishness in terms of what he calls *limit-experience,* "the response that man encounters when he has decided to put himself radically in question" (1993, 203), "the experience of what is outside the whole when the whole excludes every outside" (205). This experience is opposed to what Blanchot calls pagan life, defined by unified culture, permanent truth, and rootedness in time and place. The Jew in his perpetual diaspora represents the principle of a nomadic movement that Blanchot affirms, not as a privation but rather as "an authentic manner of residing," a way of being not bound to an eternally fixed reality, of recognizing that the truth itself is not always sedentary (127). Primitive, pagan reality ceases to suffice when it no longer holds the key to all of the relations to which human beings are subject. This opposition—in fact an often violent antipathy—between pagan rootedness and Jewish nomadism corresponds to the uneasy relation between culture and literature: "Culture tends to conceive of and to establish as relations of unity relations that, on the basis of literature, give themselves as infinite, that is, irreducible to any unifying process" (400). The Jew is thus symbolically joined to the literary as a figure of infinite movement, uncontained by a culture that seeks to unify everything and to destroy what it cannot assimilate. "Infinite movement" is Blanchot's phrase for that which is perpetually transforming itself, "contesting, challenging, obliterating itself in some other mode" (338). And no text embodies this infinite movement more radically nor embraces it more joyfully than does *Finnegans Wake*.

Lévy-Bruhl's appearance in multiple forms can thus be seen as an allegory of the nomadic relation to truth that, according to Blanchot, "maintains above what is established the right to put the distribution of space into question by appealing to the initiatives of human movement and human time" (127). This fragmentation of the personage into a series of guises dislocates him from the sedentary security of any truth rooted in place and subjects him to the transforming effects of time. Levy-Bruhl's companion in metamorphosis is the Bloom of "Circe," who is transformed respectively into a barefoot lascar, the Lord Mayor of Dublin, Emperor Leopold the First, an Elder of Zion, a mother of eight children, the Messiah, a stage Irishman, and so on. We might even see the various alter egos of Lévy-Bruhl as simply further sightings of the protean Bloom. The irony here is that in the oniric, prelogical discourse of the *Wake*, Lévy-Bruhl himself becomes subject to the phenomenon of metempsychosis he describes in his theory of primitive mentality. Joyce anthropologizes the anthropologist.

Another function of these metamorphoses is that Lévy-Bruhl's complex identity as anthropologist, professor, Jew, and mystic is being broken down into its component parts. To follow an argument made by McHugh (1976, 31), Lévy-Bruhl's manifestation as Wyndham Lewis serves Joyce's general purpose in book 1 of satirizing the manner in which the scientific spirit passes judgment on the artistic; or, to put the argument in slightly different terms, he parodies the eternal *coincidentia oppositorum* between the critical and creative faculties within the figure of the artist. At the same time, he parodies anthropology's pretensions to scientific truth in the defensive, authoritarian posturings of the professor. The agon between Shem as poet and Shaun as professor is really between two modes of discourse: one musical, plaintive, and playful; the other ponderous, doctrinaire, and rationalist to the point of hysteria. Joyce would have been attracted to Lévy-Bruhl's vision of an alternate conceptual reality but would have been wary of the epistemological violence inherent in an "anthrapologising" discourse. Like Eliot, Joyce uses the artifacts uncovered by anthropological research in constructing the *bricolage* of his own text. At the same time, however, he targets anthropology among other disciplines in his deconstruction of the forms of Western discourse. He parodies Lévy-Bruhl to his face, then goes round the back door to raid the professor's study.

IV

In their respective uses of the primitive, the difference between Eliot and Joyce can be understood in terms of a distinction Foucault makes between anthropology and ethnology as such. The former, insofar as it seeks a general concept of "man," a universal human nature, is no more than a "pious wish" (1970, 379). The "precritical analysis of what man is in his essence" is what Foucault calls the "anthropological sleep" (341). Anthropology, in other words, is a discourse, a means by which "man" represents himself to himself. In contrast to this totalizing discourse, ethnology, like psychoanalysis, "leaps over representation"; it has the capacity to analyze representation itself and the conditions within a given culture that make possible its particular forms. It "situates itself within the dimension of historicity" (376), uncovering the relations between representation and the material conditions of existence. In this critical analysis of representation, ethnology is allied with the literature that is "fascinated with the being of language" (383).

Eliot's resurrection of the primitive shares some of the "precritical" and totalizing gestures that Foucault ascribes to anthropology. Even in late essays like "Notes Towards the Definition of Culture" (1948), the primitive remains for Eliot both a legitimate object of representation and a means by which to adumbrate his vision of an ideal cultural order: permanent, organically unified, transcending history. The poet's task, he suggests in *Four Quartets*, is to create allegories of this order in a mythic representation of history: "history is a pattern / Of timeless moments" (1952, 144).

Joyce's writing shares with Foucault's idea of ethnology a critical distance on representation. The primitive is not an object of representation but is itself an ironic re-presentation: a construct embedded within the discourses of myth and history. "What a picture primitive!" (*FW* 405.3) is the cry of mock admiration at a vision of Shaun in splendid postman's array, a figure of imperial power disseminating postcard images of a pastoral, sentimentalized Ireland. Where Eliot mythologizes history, Joyce would appear in cases like this to historicize mythology. Ultimately, however, Joyce collapses both myth and history into a radical materiality of language; their modes of representation become elements in a textual field of infinite combinations that annihilates the distinction between representation and its object. For Eliot, that distance remains: the limits of language render it distinct from the object of mystical knowledge and faith; at some point along the soul's journey, language must be discarded. But Joyce refuses this limit and instead expands the universe of his language beyond any boundary yet defined.

4

Joyce, *Hamlet*, Mallarmé

In chapter 9 of Joyce's *Ulysses,* Stephen Dedalus addresses an impromptu lecture on *Hamlet* to a group of members of the Irish literary revival casually assembled in the office adjoining the main reading room of the National Library in Dublin's Kildare Street. The subject is a natural one for Stephen, who, like Hamlet, writes poetry, grieves for the recent death of a parent, dresses in mourning, and bears a certain ill will toward those around him. Stephen's melancholic character, however, does not prevent him from a dazzling display of intellect in his exposition of Shakespeare's greatest tragedy.

In his lecture, Stephen refutes the traditional notion that of all Shakespeare's characters, Hamlet is the one with whom Shakespeare himself most identifies. Instead, Stephen argues, Shakespeare has created his own image in the ghost of Hamlet's father, and the character of Hamlet really stands for Hamnet, Shakespeare's son, who died in 1596 at the age of eleven. Drawing on newly available biographical material, Stephen goes on to draw a complete series of correspondences between the characters in the play and the members of Shakespeare's family. Thus Stephen's speculations on an adulterous liaison between Shakespeare's wife, Ann, and his brother, Richard, provide the model for Gertrude and Claudius, making the Ghost into a figure for Shakespeare's own resentment and estrangement from his origins. Shakespeare's twenty-year residence in London (1592–1613)—the period of his entire dramatic career—is thus interpreted as exile from the family in Stratford toward whom he has become embittered. As Stephen says, "The note of banishment, banishment from the heart, banishment from home, sounds uninterruptedly" throughout Shakespeare's tragedy (*U* 9.1000).

As a biographical tour de force, Stephen's library lecture is as fanciful as it is sensational. For me, however, it has served as a point of departure for a reflection on the nature of performance as *mimesis,* that is, as a mode of representing nature or the truth. Beginning with Joyce's text and then moving to related discussions of the subject in modern critical theory, I propose the idea that *Hamlet* marks the beginning of a historical process in which the traditional notion of performance as mimesis is gradually subverted by a radical questioning as to the nature of the supposed object of imitation. In so doing, I willingly take the risk of lending support to Oscar Wilde's admittedly outrageous claim that when Hamlet utters "that hackneyed aphorism" about the play holding the mirror up to nature (*Hamlet* 3.2.16ff.), he is deliberately attempting "to convince the bystanders of his absolute insanity in all art-matters" (73).[1] Wilde's larger aim, of course, is to subvert the tradition of mimesis that subordinates art to some ostensibly represented truth. Art, according to Wilde, is not to be judged by any external standards of resemblance, because "art never expresses anything but itself" (80). This is the case not because art is removed from reality, but rather because the two are so intimate—our sense of reality being already a kind of art, in the sense of something made, a world constructed, as Joyce puts it, "upon the incertitude of the void" (*U* 17.1014–15).

In the library scene of *Ulysses,* Joyce approaches the subject of performance in a number of ways: there is the fact, for example, that the lecture is itself a self-conscious performance. Stephen, a young poet, has been excluded from the inner circle of the literary revival as tacit punishment for an ungenerous review he has written on the work of Augusta Gregory. Here he seeks to avenge the slight by impressing his hearers with a brilliant performance. "But act," he tells himself, "Act speech. They mock to try you. Act. Be acted on" (*U* 9.978–79). The fact that Stephen finally admits, under questioning, that he disbelieves his own theory (*U* 9.1067) merely affirms its performative nature.

The performance most important to Stephen's theory, however, is the premiere of *Hamlet* at the Globe Theatre in June 1602, in which Shakespeare himself played the role of the Ghost. Stephen recreates for his listeners the scene as Shakespeare enters the stage:

> Shakespeare who has studied *Hamlet* all the years of his life which were not vanity in order to play the part of the spectre. He speaks the words to Burbage, the young player who stands before him beyond the rack of cerecloth, calling him by a name:
>
> *Hamlet, I am thy father's spirit,*

bidding him list. To a son he speaks, the son of his soul, the prince, young Hamlet and to the son of his body, Hamnet Shakespeare, who has died in Stratford that his namesake may live forever. (*U* 9.164–73)

In other words, Shakespeare, himself a ghost by absence and estrangement from his family, plays the ghost of the dead king, and in addressing Burbage as Hamlet he is also speaking to the ghost of his dead son, Hamnet, who, had he lived, would have been seventeen in 1602, a young man like Hamlet. The ghost of the father speaks to the ghost of the son in what one might call an overdetermination of spectrality.

Now, it is not new to remark that the scene of a ghostly father returning to haunt the son has a certain resonance with Freudian theory and especially with Ernest Jones's essay on "Hamlet and the Oedipus Complex," a copy of which Joyce had acquired in Trieste (Ellmann 54). Thus Stephen is made to discourse eloquently on the pain brought by the son: "his growth is his father's decline, his youth his father's envy, his friend his father's enemy" (*U* 9.855–57). But it is perhaps less obvious to remark that Joyce also locates this rivalry in the subject himself, who in his divided condition is both father and son to himself. Stephen's theory concludes that Shakespeare is both ghost and prince, father and son in one, and thus marked internally by the same struggle that sets Hamlet and the Ghost at cross purposes. As Shakespeare is treated by Joyce as a figure of human universality, the suggestion is that for Joyce he represents the divided condition of the subject per se, whether he be Shakespeare, Hamlet, or Stephen Dedalus. Speaking of the male subject in the temporal sense, one might say that the youth is father to the older man of his own later life, while the mature man stands in the position of father to his former youth in the sense that entails rivalry, regret, and resentment—in short, castration, which is the psychoanalytic word for ghostliness.

As Mulligan says of Stephen's theory, "He proves by algebra that Hamlet's grandson is Shakespeare's grandfather and that he himself is the ghost of his own father" (*U* 1.555–57). For all his mockery, Mulligan correctly identifies the fundamental points of Stephen's discourse: the filial relations binding Hamlet (as Hamnet) to Shakespeare; Stephen's unspoken identification with both of these figures; and his failed relation with his own father, another ghost by absence whose ruined condition finds its emotional analogue in Stephen's own *aboulie,* or loss of feeling.

The question of Stephen's "search for a father" is an old one in Joyce studies, and for a long time it was given the rather superficial answer that Stephen finds a surrogate father in Bloom. This solution has been rendered unsatisfactory by both the language of Joyce and the insights of psychoanalysis concerning the perpetually vexed and doubtful nature of fatherhood. In Joyce, Stephen's relation to his father is symptomatic of the incertitude belonging to the paternal function in general. Stephen reflects that "Fatherhood, in the sense of conscious begetting, is unknown to man. It is a mystical estate, an apostolic succession from only begetter to only begotten" (U 9.837–39). Lacan himself remarks, "Ulysses is a testimony to the way in which Joyce remains caught up, rooted in his father, while still disowning and denying him. This is precisely his symptom" (1976, 15). Citing this diagnosis, Rabaté argues that for Stephen, as for Joyce, the cure lies in the son's own artistic fatherhood through the conception of the word: "if the son may have to redeem the failed father, it is not by any appeal to a symbolic father, whoever he may be, but by a deeper comprehension of the process of naming" (1988, 220–21).

Stephen acknowledges his own affiliation with the troubled relation between Hamlet père et fils by his internal remark, "He is in my father. I am in his son" (U 9.390), where "he" is Shakespeare/the Ghost and "his son" is Hamnet/Hamlet. A triple analogy is at work here: Shakespeare is to his son, Hamnet, as the ghost is to Hamlet as Stephen's father is to Stephen. In each case, the father is restless and embittered, the son melancholy and estranged from the world and himself. Stephen, in other words, sees himself in Hamlet, whom his theory identifies as Shakespeare's phantom son. When Mulligan says of Stephen that "he himself is the ghost of his own father," in one sense this merely anticipates Stephen's point that the presence of the son marks the demise of the father. But the same formula applied to Hamlet means that he is the ghost of a ghost, a figure marked by an excess of absence whose being is the sign of nonbeing.

The vision of Hamlet as double in his ghostliness is essentially that of another poetic Stephen, Mallarmé, in a text to which Joyce alludes repeatedly. At an early point in Stephen Dedalus's lecture, the assistant librarian Richard Best recalls Mallarmé's description of Hamlet as "lisant au livre de lui-même" [reading in the book of himself] and of a performance of the play in a provincial French town, where it was advertised as Hamlet, ou le Distrait: Pièce de Shakespeare. This intervention, presented as a casual association in the speech of a minor character, in fact provides the basic elements of Joyce's preoccupation with Shakespeare's play. These include the presence of a "French" *Hamlet* along with the entire cult of *Hamletisme* represented here by Stephen, recently returned from Paris. The figure of Hamlet reading the book of himself conforms to Mallarmé's definition of *Hamlet* as *the* play, as the prototype of the "théatre de notre esprit" (300) [theatre of our mind], or the "drame avec Soi" [drama of the subject], which in Shakespeare's work superseded the older play of multiple action. It further identifies Hamlet in his act of self-reading as a "haut et vivant Signe" [a high and living Sign]—Mallarmé here insisting on Hamlet's preeminently semiotic and hermeneutic functions, on the lofty and noble sign made by the act of deciphering the self. Finally, and in the immediate context of the exchange taking place in the reading room of the National Library, this series of allusions leads Stephen to recall Mallarmé's description of the play's ending as a "sumptuous and stagnant exaggeration of murder" (*U* 9.129). Stephen is preoccupied, in other words, by the lugubrious rhythms of Mallarmé's language as well as by the notion of the play as a performance of excess, a ritual and hyperbolic repetition.

The lines cited by Joyce are from Mallarmé's note to his own more substantial piece on *Hamlet*, inspired by Mounet-Sully's performance in the title role at the Comédie Française in 1886. Where Stephen sees Shakespeare doubled as ghost and prince, Mallarmé sees Hamlet himself as a ghostly double, as both "le seigneur latent qui ne peut devenir" [the noble lord of unfulfilled promise] and "juvénile ombre de tous" [the young shade of us all]. Hamlet, in other words, is twice ghostly, representing both the ghost of the father, the king he will never become, and also the ghost of the son, the shade in all of us of squandered promise and lost occasions. This double nature of Hamlet—at once son and father, here and elsewhere, present and absent—leads Mallarmé to consider him as a character best played in a ghostly manner.

Mallarmé's Hamlet, the one he has seen performed so much to his liking by Mounet-Sully, has what the poet calls a nameless quality of "effacement subtil et fané" [subtle and faded effacement], "une imagerie de jadis" [imagery of yesteryear], which is missing from the work of certain artists "aimant à représenter un fait comme il en arrive, clair, battant neuf!" [who like to represent a fact as it first occurs, clear and brand new!]. For Mallarmé's taste, the customary style of the *Théâtre français* makes things overly vivid; it falsifies by throwing life too much into relief. This pernicious influence is purged from the stage by Mounet-Sully's Hamlet, a figure who appears as a stranger everywhere, and everywhere imposes that nameless, faded quality through "l'inquiétant ou funèbre envahissement de sa présence" [the disquieting and funereal invasion of his presence] (302).

With this evocation of Hamlet as a faded and fading presence, Mallarmé stands squarely within a modern critical tradition that is devoted to the "fading of the subject" and that later ranges from Jones and Freud through Lacan, Barthes, and Derrida. As Ned Lukacher writes in his account of this critical phenomenon, "'fading' describes the negativity inherent in the subject" (72). The Platonic idea of a subject made wholly present to himself and to others through voice and gesture—in short, through performance—has faded and is gradually being replaced by the notion of voice or performance not as the outward expression or the mask of a presence but rather as the concealment of something missing. What Barthes calls the "tonal instability" of narrative voice, or "*le fading des voix*" in modern writing, testifies to this fading of the subject as well. For Mallarmé, then, the brilliance of Mounet-Sully's performance lies in his capacity to convey this sense of the faded subject on stage—to perform the character of Hamlet as a kind of phantom presence "qui se débat sous le mal d'apparaître" (299) [who struggles against the curse of having to appear]. A good deal of the enigma of Hamlet, as well as his attractiveness as a representative figure of the modern subject, has to do with the inherent negativity of his dramatic function, which may be variously characterized as the power of impotence, the act of inaction, and the performance of nonperformance.

In order to explore the idea of Hamlet's ghostliness as having historical meaning, I turn to a remark made by Benjamin in his essay "On the Mimetic Faculty," which is in effect a theory of the history of performance. In this essay, Benjamin identifies the mimetic faculty as a "powerful compulsion" belonging to the earliest stages of human history—a compulsion "to become and behave like something else" (1986, 333). In ancient times this faculty, as expressed in dance, for example, performed the function of affirming the resemblances or correspondences between microcosm and macrocosm, or between the perceptible world and the world beyond human perception. The modern world, however, has witnessed "the increasing decay of the mimetic faculty" because "the observable world of modern man contains only minimal residues of the magical correspondences and analogies that were familiar to ancient peoples" (334).

The origins of performance, according to this definition, would lie in the mimesis of unseen powers and presences reenacted or represented in ritual dance and other forms of cultic practice. In Benjamin's version of the history of mimesis, the element of magic in ritual practice is dissolved when this practice is superseded by writing, which establishes its relations according to a semiotic system that is not inherently mimetic. This account of the fading of the mimetic power echoes that of Benjamin's better-known essay "The Work of Art in the Age of Mechanical Reproduction," where he finds that the original value of art, conferred by its function in ritual and cultic practice, has suffered a decay in the modern age. For Benjamin, the turning point in this process of art's estrangement from its original mimetic object occurs in the Renaissance, when art is suddenly released from its ritual context in magic and religion (1969, 22).

We have already witnessed Mallarmé's observation that *Hamlet* marks a transition in Shakespeare's own work between the drama of multiple action and the drama of the self. But the additional perspective provided by Benjamin offers a much greater historical scale on which to measure the play. Benjamin's theory enables one to locate *Hamlet* at a transitional stage between ritualistic and symbolic practice, or between the mimesis of the supernatural (here represented by the Ghost) and the mimesis of the self (represented by the character Hamlet). Shakespeare's play, in other words, registers the interiorization of mimesis, in which the mysteries formerly accorded to unseen powers in heaven or, in any case, beyond the grave, are now reformulated as mysteries of human motivation and action. Only in *Hamlet* this process of reformulation is not complete: the new human drama of self-representation has not wholly displaced the older drama of man's relation to the supernatural, so that the two take place side by side, vying for control of the stage in a play itself bound "to double business" (3.3.41).

This state of affairs, where two rival modes of performance stand in suspension, would account for the infamous instability of the play remarked upon, for example, in Eliot's observation that *Hamlet* is "superposed upon much cruder material which persists even in the final form" (1975, 46). Eliot here refers specifically to the textual problem of the play as an incomplete revision of an older, now lost play by Thomas Kyd. But his uneasiness is also occasioned by a feeling of bafflement in interpreting the ontological status of the ghostly apparition of Hamlet's father. Is the Ghost real, as it indeed seems to Hamlet when in act 1 its presence is witnessed by himself and three other persons? Is it unreal, as Hamlet suggests in act 2, attributing the apparition to "my own weakness and my melancholy" (2.2.587)? Or is it perhaps something between the real and the unreal, as it seems in act 3 when Hamlet discourses with the Ghost in the presence of his mother, who sees "nothing at all" of the Ghost, "yet all that is I see" (3.4.133)? On one hand, Hamlet's bafflement is a crisis of doubt as to whether the Ghost is external or internal to himself. On the other hand, the Queen's confidence that "all that is I see" belongs to the wholly observable world of modern man that the play itself hesitates to enter. It hesitates because the modern world heralded by the Renaissance is only apparently observable—its mysteries are now buried within the human subject or within the nature of events themselves. Shakespeare's play appears to mark this shift in the locus of mystery even in the structure of its action, which moves from the older material of the revenge tragedy—with its obedience to the supernatural—to the new material of inner motivation. The precise moment of this shift in fact may occur with Hamlet's defiance of augury at 5.2.208ff. When Horatio warns him against accepting the challenge to a fencing match with Laertes, Hamlet refuses to put it off: "Not a whit. We defy augury. There is special providence in the fall of a sparrow. . . . Since no man knows of aught he leaves, what is't to leave betimes? Let be." Hamlet's acceptance of his unknown fate reflects a newfound alacrity and readiness for whatever may come. He himself thus represents the interiorization of an unfathomable abyss whose outward and more ancient manifestation is the Ghost: "But thou wouldst not think how ill all's here about my heart. But it is no matter." (5.2.206) It doesn't matter, but it is also no matter: not something material, not the black bile that Robert Burton diagnoses as the cause of melancholy, it is something else, something other, an absence about the heart. This displacement of the ghostly function onto Hamlet himself—marking the subject with the negativity of "not being" invoked in Hamlet's famous soliloquy—is what makes it possible for the Ghost to be identified both with Hamlet, as in the case of Mallarmé, and with Shakespeare, as in the case of Joyce. In these respective discourses, both Hamlet and Shakespeare serve as names for the interiority of absence.

When the object of mimesis is internalized, performance becomes a mimesis of the self. But in this very process the duality of mimesis, which requires both an object and its imitation, is compromised. For how exactly do we imitate ourselves, except through a kind of performance that is indistinguishable from its object? This is essentially the question posed by Derrida concerning the prose piece *Mimique*, Mallarmé's meditation on a pantomime by Paul Margueritte, published alongside his review of Mounet-Sully's Hamlet in October 1886. Margueritte's bizarre and haunting spectacle, entitled *Pierrot assassin de sa femme*, takes the form of a mimed confession in which the traditional comedic personage has become diabolical; he shows how he murdered the beautiful Colombine by a method that leaves no incriminating evidence: he has tickled her to death. Margueritte's published version of the piece has the mime reenacting the role of victim as well as torturer:

> Elle (il) éclate d'un rire vrai, strident, mortel; et se dresse à mi-corps; et veut se jeter hors du lit; et toujours ses pieds dansent, chatouillés, torturés, épileptiques. C'est l'agonie. (18)

> [She (he) bursts out in a real laugh, strident and mortal; she (he) sits up, trying to throw herself from the bed; and still her (his) feet are dancing, tickled, tortured, epileptic. It's agony.]

No sooner has he relived the murder than the spasms that killed Colombine now convulse Pierrot's own body. In desperate hilarity, he drinks himself to death: "Il glisse spectral, déjà mort" (22) [He glides as a spectre, already dead].

Mallarmé finds in this piece a spectral and dreamlike ambiguity on the level of signification—it puts into play a series of gestures that have all the formal characteristics of signifiers, yet that always stop short of signifying a real object or action. Mimesis, then, without a decidable object. Mallarmé, however, finds precisely in the undecidable object of mimesis not a failure of signification but rather a medium of pure fiction (in the sense of *fictio*, a making) that stands outside the logic of truth and its imitation, reality and its representation: "Tel opère le mime, dont le jeu se borne à une allusion perpétuelle sans briser la glace: il installe, ainsi, un milieu, pur, de fiction" (310) [That is how the mime operates, whose act is confined to a perpetual allusion without breaking the ice or the mirror: he thus sets up a medium, a pure medium, of fiction].

Derrida places Mallarmé's essay next to a passage from Plato's *Philebus* that establishes the traditional logic of mimesis as the imitation or representation of a decidable truth (*logos*). In illustrating this principle, Plato compares the soul to a book in which truth itself is more or less truthfully rendered. This is of course the same figure that Hamlet uses in his promise to "remember" the Ghost:

> And thy commandment all alone shall live
> Within the book and volume of my brain.
> (1.5.102–3)

It is also Mallarmé's figure for Hamlet, "lisant au livre de lui-même" [reading in the book of himself]. In any case, the juxtaposition of Plato's dialogue with Mallarmé's *Mimique* provides Derrida with the occasion for a "double session" on these two texts, between which lies an entire history of the relation between literature and truth or, if you will, between performance and its object. During the course of this history the mimetic function has not so much lost its power as it has lost a certain ontological grounding insofar as the object of mimesis, no longer rooted in the Platonic *logos*, has been cast adrift. Derrida writes of the pantomime evoked by Mallarmé that it "no longer belongs to the system of truth, does not manifest, produce, or unveil any presence; it does not constitute any conformity, resemblance, or adequation between a presence and a representation." Again, "The plays of facial expression and the gestural tracings are not present in themselves since they always refer, perpetually allude or represent. But they don't represent anything that has ever been or can ever become present" (1991, 183–84). The purely gestural nature of this performance calls to mind a remark made by Benjamin on Kafka. Benjamin observes that the central element of Kafka's work is the gesture—the exaggerated gesture without apparent motivation that does not signify anything but itself: "Each gesture is an event—one might even say, a drama—in itself" (1969, 121).

The haunting nature of this gestural excess is what Eliot observes in *Hamlet* when he says of the play and of himself that "the intense feeling, ecstatic or terrible, without an object or exceeding its object, is something that every person of sensibility has known" (1975, 49). And it is precisely this aspect of the play that haunts Stephen Dedalus when he recalls Mallarmé's description of *Hamlet* as a "sumptuous and stagnant exaggeration of murder" (*U* 9.129). The isolation of this citation in Joyce's text suggests that he as well as Mallarmé has reflected on the excessive morbidity of Shakespeare's play. Murder here lacks the economy of motivation that it has in, say, *Julius Caesar:* Polonius, Ophelia, Rosencrantz and Guildenstern, Laertes, the Queen, the King, Hamlet himself—this surplus of corpses strewn about seems but the extension of Hamlet's own funereal presence from the moment that he first casts his shadow on the stage.

If for Mallarmé it is Hamlet who is the real ghost, Joyce carries this logic merely one step further in making Shakespeare himself the ghost, who, on the stage of the Globe, addresses the ghost of his son, Hamnet. Displaced, in Stephen's discourse, from the figure of Hamlet himself onto that of the absent father addressing the absent son, Shakespeare is seen as performing the condition of his own radical absence and, by extension, as enacting the nature of existence itself as a kind of haunting. In Joyce's logic, identification with the ghost has become a condition of authorship.

That is, Shakespeare's identification with the Ghost of Hamlet's father becomes a figure for Joyce of the ghostliness of authorship in general, as well as of other forms of artistic performance. In an aspect of Joyce's work that will be more fully explored in the work of Beckett, the performance itself arises out of the radical awareness that there is nothing behind it; that nothing is being performed; that what is being performed is precisely that nothingness. Whatever one might make of this situation in Beckett, one need not see it as a gesture of nihilism on Joyce's part; it is rather an affirmation of a performance that, like life—*as* life—no longer belongs to a logic of mimesis that insists on the duality of truth and its representation. Having been released by the Renaissance from its ritual context in magic and religion, the art of performance now secures its final and more terrifying freedom—a release from the system of truth itself.

5

Scenes of Reading

In Paul Auster's *City of Glass,* there is a writer who, while in the waiting room of in a train station, finds himself sitting next to a girl chewing gum and reading one of his novels. Without identifying himself as the author, he eagerly solicits her judgment of the work. She replies with a shrug, "It passes the time, I guess. Anyway, it's no big deal. It's just a book" (65). One can imagine a similar fate for *City of Glass.* Auster satirizes at once the vanity of the author, the indifference of the reader, and the unpredictable manner in which the text may be put to uses less exalted than those for which it was intended. At this point we are not exactly outside the text. But we are at least at a point in the text where its outside, and its fate on the outside, is imagined. Indeed a characteristic feature of the literary text in the twentieth century is this preemptive strike at reception, this tactic of including within the content of the text the range of possible interpretations to which the text might be subjected. It is a strategy that often takes the form of representing within the frame of the text—whether ironically or in some other mode—the scene in which the text is to be read.

Here, then, I suggest, is one way of approaching the limits of textuality. Such scenes of reading in literature can serve as material for reflection on the nature of reading as a cultural practice, in part because they attempt to define the time and space of reading. Beyond this, the literary representation of reading is one way literature defines itself and even foresees its own destiny in the reader's hands, which is to say in the world beyond the text. As Walter Benjamin reminds us, books have their fates (1969, 61). The limits of the text would be found, in this sense, at precisely those points where the text conceives of itself, or of any other text, as an object sent forth into a material world beyond its own boundaries. At issue here is the larger question of how the form of a literary text is related to reading practices, either as it is determined by existing conventions of reading, or as it resists such conventions and seeks to impose new kinds of reading.

The preoccupation of the literary text with the problem of its own limits is symptomatic of a historical moment of radical uncertainty concerning both the practice of reading and the nature of the reading public. This
moment, I suggest, belongs particularly if not uniquely to the twentieth
century. Reading in the nineteenth century was more likely to be considered a mode of participation in an activity of public dimensions, national
importance, and historical meaning. Even so deeply personal a poem as
Keats's "On First Looking into Chapman's Homer" is written in such a
way as to suggest the importance of reading to a collective human polity.
The poet's own history as a reader is rendered as a knowledge of "states
and kingdoms," while its final vision—of Spanish explorers gathered on
the edge of the Pacific—relies on an image of collective endeavor and discovery:

Then felt I like some watcher of the skies
When a new planet swims into his ken;
Or like stout Cortez when with eagle eyes
He star'd at the Pacific—and all his men
Look'd at each other with wild surmise—
Silent, upon a peak in Darien.

In comparing his personal experience as a reader to the great discoveries
of science and geographical exploration, Keats redefines reading as an act
of historical as well as personal significance. Three things happen in the
poem: first, reading serves to unveil the realm of the sublime and so belongs to a romantic repertoire of the means to such unveilings; second, a
privileged instance of reading creates an irreversible transformation in the
life of the subject, who will never again be the same; and finally, both this
unveiling and this transformation are implicitly assigned to a more general historical moment: a "subjective turn" that makes of subjectivity itself
the next great field of exploration, the path to whose discovery lies
through the literary text, as written and read.

The nineteenth-century novel, like the lyric poem, was written for a
broad-based, national readership. In form and subject matter, it implied a
collective public imagination and a society unified by the act of reading.
Although this preoccupation with cultural unity forged through a common experience of reading is commonly associated with the name of Matthew Arnold, it was shared by Victorian writers as different in sensibility
as Dickens and Ruskin. Dickens not only wrote very deliberately for a national audience, but he exhausted himself in public readings in the belief

that he was establishing harmony among the social classes by creating a single culture of readers (Small 275). Ruskin's most popular book, *Sesame and Lilies* (1865), originally took the form of a public address urging the support of public libraries, a project designed to alleviate the distressed condition of the people by offering them the neglected treasures of the book. Ruskin sees the book as the common reader's introduction to an exclusive society, an invitation to enter into conversation with the great and noble minds of the cultural pantheon. In terms of the politics of culture, this philanthropic project represents a means of pacifying the forces of social unrest by redistributing the cultural capital in order to create, in theory at least, a sense of unity among the classes through the establishment of a shared cultural heritage.

The literary modernists of the twentieth century simply do not share this vision of a unified reading public, either as a social reality or as a desired objective in the writing of literary texts. Rather, they find themselves responding to a condition that Wlad Godzich has described as a "new heterogeneity in the culture of literacy," part of an economic climate where increasing specialization in the production of goods and services leads to a corresponding elaboration of linguistic codes, such as those of medicine and law, and later, those of politics and literary criticism (8). To this list of newly elaborated codes I would add literary modernism.

The language of modernism is not only predicated on the breakup of a unified reading public; it also reflects a crisis in the representation of reading. Mallarmé's line, "La chair est triste, hélas, et j'ai lu tous les livres," [The flesh is sad, alas, and I've read all the books] (in *Brise marine*, 1865) is echoed sixty-eight years later by Gertrude Stein's avowed fear that her voracious reading would exhaust a limited supply of books worthy to be read, and that eventually she would reach a point when "there would be nothing unread to read" (68). These remarks belong to a more general thematic in modernism devoted to what one might call the end of reading, or the death of the reader as such, of the figure summoned up by both Keats and Ruskin who masters heroically the distances between the reader's subjective experience, the national historical moment, and the eternal values of a classical pantheon.

The modernist revision of the scene of reading may be traced to Proust's 1905 preface to his translation of Ruskin, where the Victorian writer's heroic vision is subjected to an ironic turn. Proust hears in Ruskin a muted echo of the Enlightenment and particularly of Descartes, for whom "la lecture de tous les bons livres est comme une conversation avec les plus honnêtes gens des siècles passés qui en ont été les auteurs" [the reading of all good books is like a conversation with those who have been writers among the best people of centuries past]. This is the thought one finds throughout Ruskin's essay, "enveloppée seulement dans un or apollonien où fondent des brumes anglaises, pareil à celui dont la gloire illumine les paysages de son peintre préféré" (Proust 1987, 61) [only enveloped in an Apollonian gold dissolved in English fog, like the one that gloriously illuminates the landscapes of his favorite painter].

Seeing through the Turneresque fog of Ruskin's thinking, Proust arrives at a different idea of reading. "La lecture, au rebours de la conversation, [consiste] pour chacun de nous à recevoir communication d'une autre pensée, mais tout en restant seul, c'est-à-dire en continuant à jouir de la puissance intellectuelle qu'on a dans la solitude et que la conversation dissipe immédiatement" (1987, 62) [Reading, unlike conversation, consists for each of us in receiving the communication of another's thought while yet remaining alone, that is while continuing to enjoy the intellectual power one has in solitude and which conversation immediately dissipates].

In this definition, Proust distances himself at once from the rationalism of the Enlightenment, from bourgeois good intentions, and from fin-de-siècle decadence. Rather, he seeks to redefine reading in a way that addresses the specific predicament of the modern subject—that of restoring a sense of personal unity by reconciling his own present and past. But unlike Ruskin's, this is a very private project for Proust, one to which conversation can only serve as a distraction. The very idea of a national culture, to say nothing of such a culture being defined by a collective polity of readers, has been thoroughly discredited by the Dreyfus affair. On the contrary, Proust defines the reader precisely as one removed from the public sphere.

Proust is the first modern writer to explore in detail the time and space of reading in such a way as to redefine the practice in a specifically modern context. On one hand, reading occurs in Proust as a ritualized invocation of the spirit of solitude, a privileged moment rescued from the deteriorating scene of modernity. On the other hand, the act of reading bears the signs of a dying art, and Proust writes a kind of elegy for the romantic experience we have witnessed in Keats, of reading as an unveiling of the sublime, as an irreversible transformation of the subject, and as the defining practice of a new moment in history. In his very celebration of reading in its occult and ritualized nature, Proust implicitly acknowledges that the romantic mode of reading is no longer possible, neither for his narrator nor for twentieth-century life. Reading becomes more precious and rarefied for Proust insofar as it is understood as an endangered species of experience.

Proust's elegy for the "lost time" of reading can itself be read in three distinct scenes occurring in the beginning, middle, and final volumes of *A la recherche du temps perdu*. The first of these scenes is one that Proust's narrator recalls from his childhood summers at Combray, where he would pass long hours reading, often in bed, in tomblike solitude behind shutters closed against the afternoon sun. Sent outside for the sake of his health, the child seeks refuge in the garden shed, where the act of reading distorts his awareness of the passing of time marked by the church bells of Saint-Hilaire. "A chaque heure il me semblait que c'était quelques instants seulement auparavant que la précédente avait sonné" [as each hour struck, it would seem to me that a few moments only had passed since the hour before]:

> Quelquefois même cette heure prématurée sonnait deux coups de plus que la dernière; il y en avait donc une que je n'avais pas entendue, quelque chose qui avait eu lieu n'avait pas eu lieu pour moi; l'interêt de la lecture, magique comme un profond sommeil, avait donné le change à mes oreilles hallucinés et effacé la cloche d'or sur la surface azurée du silence. (1.87)

> [Sometimes it would happen that this precious hour would sound two strokes more than the last; there must then have been an hour which I had not heard strike; something that had taken place had not taken place for me; the fascination had deceived my enchanted ears and had obliterated the sound of that golden bell from the azure surface of the enveloping silence.] (1.94)

The passage, as told by a narrator who no longer experiences reading in this way, remembers nostalgically a readerly life lived in concealment and in pleasurable indifference to the surrounding world of servants and of troops passing in the streets—indifference, that is, to the world of work and war. The passage renders homage to the lost time of reading, but it nonetheless makes clear that reading takes place outside of life; indeed, it constitutes a kind of antithesis to the more lively, active hermeneutic that the narrator will finally recognize as essential to his vocation as a writer. The point has been made by Antoine Compagnon, who has demonstrated the many ways in which Proust condemns reading as an idolatry of the letter leading to the death of the spirit. In contrast to the antiquarianism of

Ruskin, Proust sees a library as a great cemetery, a monument to the fetishism of the book. For Proust there is death in books and death by books (Compagnon 224).

It is in this light that one might reread the famous passage in which Proust's narrator is transfixed—as if by the face of Medusa—by the scene of his grandmother reading. The episode brings together Proust's phenomenology of reading with that of the uncanny, that is, with that of the characteristically modern experience documented by Freud, in which ordinary objects and familiar faces suddenly go strange; both haunted and haunting, they expose the reality of their own death and ours. The episode begins as the narrator makes a telephone call from Doncières to his grandmother in Paris. On hearing his grandmother's voice through this fragile long-distance connection, he is struck by how it sounds in isolation from her actual presence and from the familiar sight of her face. It seems as if he is hearing this voice for the first time. It has for him an impalpable, phantomlike quality in which he seems to hear already the ghostly voice that will perhaps visit him when she is dead. The telephone connection is unexpectedly cut off, and the narrator calls in vain to his grandmother though the night, knowing that she must be doing the same from her end. His anguish anticipates the finality of that day when she will no longer be able to answer his call, and it seems to him that he has already lost her among the shadows.

Seized by the desire to see her, he makes the journey to Paris, only to behold her once more as a phantom. On entering his grandmother's salon, he comes upon her reading her cherished Mme de Sévigné, so that for a moment she is unaware of his presence, and he himself is suddenly present at the scene of his own absence. This time the feeling of strangeness comes from the sight of his grandmother abandoned to thoughts that do not concern him. For the first time he sees her from a cruelly detached perspective:

> j'aperçus sur le canapé, sous la lampe, rouge, lourde et vulgaire, malade, rêvassant, promenant au-dessus d'un livre des yeux un peu fous, une vieille femme accablée que je ne connaissais pas. (2.440)

> [I saw, sitting on the sofa beneath the lamp, red-faced, heavy and vulgar, sick, vacant, letting her slightly crazed eyes wander over a book, a dejected old woman I did not know.] (2.143)

The two scenes that make up this extraordinary episode offer alternating versions of the uncanny. In the first scene, the disembodied voice on the telephone serves as a technological counterpart to the traditional dis-embodied spirit, Proust finding a new way to be haunted in the mysterious instruments of modern communication. In the second scene, the machinery of the uncanny shifts from the auditory to the visual. Here the narrator sees his grandmother, as he says, as if in a photograph, that is, in the ruthlessly objective way that a snapshot captures its subject unaware. Unlike the human eye, which beholds its object in time and within a framework of thought and feeling, the photograph uncovers without sentiment the frank materiality of its object. Thus when Marcel is granted the ambiguous privilege of seeing his grandmother with a photographic eye, she appears to him in all her finite corporality: heavy, vulgar, sick, and vacant, an old woman he doesn't know.

For Samuel Beckett, this episode lies at the heart of Proust's analysis of the way human consciousness seeks to compensate for the losses inflicted by time. Proust's narrator sees the old woman before him as a stranger because, anxious and fatigued by his journey, he allows his habitually tender regard to fall into abeyance. He suddenly sees that the familiar person of his customary affection is a creature surviving only in his memory, and that this cherished grandmother of the past has in fact long been dead (1931, 15). For all that he might wish for the old illusion to regain its habitual sway, his grandmother will never again be more than a ghost of the person he remembers. Most familiar to readers of Proust is his theory of involuntary memory, of the incident or object that unexpectedly recovers a past beyond the reach of conscious attempts at remembrance. Proust's version of the uncanny is but the negative image of such an experience. In this case, a chance incident recovers not a past lost in the shadows of time but rather the terrifying present that a sentimental memory has obscured. The power of the uncanny is both verified and rendered transparent by Proust's capacity to think it through as a return of the repressed, to reveal its sources and consequences in the evolving forms of human consciousness.

The scene also belongs, however, to the logic of Proust's necromancy of reading. The narrator suddenly sees his beloved grandmother in her gross corporeality, so that the act of reading is rendered excessively material and physical, as the automatic movement of a dying body. When one considers, moreover, the historical specificity of the character of the grandmother—her devotion to Mme de Sévigné combined with her uneasy relation to the world of telephones and photographs—it is possible to see the scene as

Proust's emblem of the death of the reader as a certain kind of historical figure.

Near the end of Proust's work, a final scene of reading—or rather of reading's impossibility—makes the narrator painfully aware of his own mortality. Retained for a few moments in the library of the Prince de Guermantes, he takes down a copy of George Sand's *François le Champi*, one of his favorite books as a child. Only now he is unable to find any pleasure in the book, because it calls forth the child he was once, but who is now a stranger to him. The book, he feels, can only be read by this phantom of a child and not by the aged man who holds it in his hand: "immédiatement en moi un enfant se lève qui prend ma place, qui seul a le droit de lire ce titre: *François le Champi*" (4.464) [immediately there rises within me a child who takes my place, who alone has the right to spell out the title *Francois le Champi* (3.921)]. Far from being remembered fondly, this child is "l'étranger qui venait me faire mal" (4.462) [this stranger who was coming to trouble me (3.919)] to supplant and exclude him from the innocent pleasures of the book. The narrator finds himself on the losing side of an Oedipal conflict, not with his child but with the child he was, the ghost of his former self. He can no longer read, not merely because he is haunted by the reader he was, but also because the world in which a certain kind of reading could take place has passed out of existence. He understands now that in order to write he must turn away from the world of books and seek to read instead the mysterious text of his own life, that "livre intérieur de signes inconnus" (4.458) [inner book of unknown symbols (3.913)].

One might well ask how Proust envisioned the fate of his own work in a world where reading had become so problematic. Against a nineteenth-century novelistic tradition dominated by the art of narrative, he offered a text that seemed without narrative restraint and that was written in a mode that relied on subjective impression as the sole measure of internal and external reality. In renouncing this tradition, Proust was also implicitly renouncing its claims to a transparent and coherent structural unity. The material that became his great fictional work retains much of its original character as a collection of the heterogeneous pieces that Proust described in 1908 as his various projects: a study of the nobility, a Parisian novel, an essay on Sainte-Beuve and Flaubert, an essay on women, an essay on homosexuality, a study of stained glass windows, a study of tombstones, a study of the novel (*Correspondance* 8.112–13). It is no wonder that, in the second decade of the twentieth century, even some of the most sensitive readers found Proust's work unreadable. Rejecting it for publication by the *Nouvelle Revue Française* in 1913, André Gide merely skimmed the manuscript, put off by the long sentences and by the author's seemingly endless ratiocinations (Diesbach 508).

No one was more acutely aware than Proust himself of his work's illegibility given the conventions of reading practice. In the course of its composition he had proposed to read it aloud to a group of friends, but he had to give up the idea because of its length and above all the length of sentences (Diesbach 453), which exceeded the limits of his already fragile respiratory system. Proust's is the first novel in French that cannot physically be read aloud, and by this fact alone it forces a transformation in the *teknè* even of silent reading. Proust writes to a friend, Prince Antoine Bibesco, that the composition of his work is "très stricte, mais d'un ordre trop complexe pour être d'abord perceptible" (Diesbach 502) [very disciplined, but of an order too complex to be immediately perceived]. The first version (1913) was not published until Proust himself proposed to pay Bernard Grasset the costs of printing and advertising. When Gaston Gallimard's *NRF* finally agreed to publish the completed version in 1920–21, Proust had found the right audience. The *NRF* group was an intellectual élite that Proust judged to be most favorable to "the maturation and dissemination" of the ideas contained in his book. He knew that the unified public for which George Sand wrote no longer existed. The fragmentation of this public necessarily limited the readership of a writer like Proust, but it also created the conditions for literary modernism; that is, the very heterogeneity of the new reading public made it possible to rewrite the conventions of reading and to find an audience among those who were willing to accept them. It was perhaps inevitable that the works of literary modernism should merely intensify the differences in readership that had formed the conditions of their possibility, a situation that would eventually be institutionalized by the teaching of modern literature as part of a standard university education. Joyce himself would remark infamously, "My immortality does not lie through the reader but through generations of professors" (Fitch 356).

* * *

It is instructive to compare Proust to Joyce, for the two writers stand in symmetrical relation to each other. Proust is the modern writer who recovers the inner unity of the subject through a detailed observation of the social universe; Joyce is the one who reveals the outward forms of modern culture through their impressions on the inner consciousness of the subject. Apart from this, there are a number of historical parallels between *A la recherche du temps perdu* and *Ulysses*. Both works were written during the decade 1910–20; both were published in fragmentary episodes that only gradually took form as an ensemble; both found their publication hindered by their perceived indecency and by the fact that neither was written in conventionally novelistic form; and both were published in Paris, under extraordinary conditions, within a year of each other. Finally, both writers, meeting for the only time at a dinner at the Ritz in 1922, claimed politely not to have read the other's work (Ellmann 508).

As for the scene of reading, if Proust writes its elegy amid the newly heterogeneous conditions of modernity, then Joyce's way of reviving it is to incorporate these same conditions within the form of the text itself, thus ensuring its survival in the fragmented environment of reading in the twentieth century. In *Ulysses,* the scene of reading is multiplied in an endless variety of interpretive moments embedded within the fabric of daily life. Reading is not, as in Proust, set apart as a ritualized invocation of the spirit of solitude. Rather, Joyce effaces the boundaries dividing the time and space of reading from the rest of life, drawing attention to its radical materiality, its relation to bodily enjoyment, its integration into the rhythms of the city, its haptic, aleatory, transitory, and fragmentary qualities.

In this explosion of the scene of reading onto the cultural landscape of modernity, readers in Joyce (that is, fictional characters portrayed in the act of reading) consume and are consumed by banal advertisements, pompous editorials, sensational headlines, ladies' magazines, physical exercise manuals, exotic postcards, pornographic novels, obscene letters, suicide notes, and throwaway flyers announcing the coming of Elijah. Such scenes are freely combined with allusions to an immense range of texts representing the entire range of the Western literary, philosophical, and religious traditions, from Shakespeare to Wilde, from Aristotle to Marx, from the Haggadah to the Roman Catholic burial service. The effect of this integration of trivial reading with the classical tradition is not the debasement of the canon but rather the universalization of reading as a hermeneutic devoted to the forms of modern culture.

The note of heterogeneity in reading is struck at an early point in Joyce's novel, where Stephen Dedalus walks along Sandymount Strand and sees the "Signatures of all things I am here to read, seaspawn and seawrack, the nearing tide, that rusty boot (*U* 3.2–3). The allusion is to the seventeenth-century *Signatura rerum* of Jakob Boehme, but closer to Stephen's own time and romantic consciousness is Whitman, whose walks on the shores of Paumonok likewise evoke a hermeneutic of debris: "I too but signify at the utmost a little wash'd-up drift" (Whitman 202). However, Stephen's disjointed reading of the landscape belongs finally to a different order, failing to achieve the older poet's unified vision. The dispersed and fragmentary objects of Stephen's perception are a direct extension of his habit as a reader of books of "[r]eading two pages apiece of seven books every night" (*U* 2.136). Of all the characters in *Ulysses*, Stephen is the only one who could conceivably read *Ulysses* itself, and in the scattered nature of his reading Joyce mocks the discontinuities of his own work, a work of such loosely drifting sequence that narrative progress can only be measured by the time of day, a work composed of eighteen episodes written in nearly as many different styles. In this respect, reading *Ulysses* is a little like reading two pages apiece of seven books.

The form of *Ulysses*, as well as the kind of imposition it makes on the reader, is further parodied in the "Circe" episode, which Proust would describe privately, despite his professed ignorance of Joyce's work, as "magnificent, a new Inferno in full sail" (Ellmann 508). A major part of this Joycean Walpurgisnacht is devoted to a hallucinatory criminal trial of Leopold Bloom. When asked to name his profession, Bloom poses as Mr. Philip Beaufoy of the Playgoers' Club, London, a writer of popular fiction. While relieving his bowels earlier in the day, Bloom has read one of Beaufoy's stories and has torn pages from it in order to wipe himself. The scene is one of many in Joyce where the act of reading is quite physically combined with the functions of the body, whether excremental or erotic. In his guise as Beaufoy, Bloom claims to have invented a new collection of prize stories, "something that is an entirely new departure" (*U* 15.803), and accuses Bloom himself of having plagiarized some of his best-selling copy, "really gorgeous stuff, the love passages in which are beneath suspicion" (*U* 15.824). A more precise account of Bloom's compositions, however, are testified to by a Mrs. Bellingham, a society matron who claims to have received obscene letters from him:

He addressed me in several handwritings with fulsome compliments as a Venus in furs. . . . He implored me to soil his letter in an unspeakable manner, to chastise him as he richly deserves, to bestride and ride him, to give him a most vicious horsewhipping. (*U* 15.1045–73)

Apart from the allusion to Sacher-Masoch's novel *Venus im Pelz*, also satirized here is the indignant reception of Joyce's work by an American lady of the same social class as the fictional Mrs. Bellingham. While Joyce was writing the "Circe" episode in the summer of 1920, the American magazine the *Little Review* printed the "Nausicaa" episode as part of its serial publication of Joyce's novel. This is the episode that culminates with Bloom masturbating into his trousers at Gertie MacDowell's erotic exhibition of her underthings. In an attempt to attract new subscribers, the issue of the *Little Review* with this episode was sent unsolicited to some readers, including the daughter of a prominent New York attorney. This person found the material offensive and turned it over to her father with the demand that the magazine be prosecuted for obscenity (Vanderham 37). The result was a legal ban on the publication of *Ulysses* in the United States, which remained in effect until overturned more than a decade later by the U.S. District Court.

The Mrs. Bellingham of "Circe" has certain things in common with the New York attorney's daughter: both represent the bourgeois morality that was officially embodied in the New York Society for the Suppression of Vice; both receive the offending reading matter as unsolicited mail; both turn their personal indignation into a case for legal prosecution. In the trial of Bloom as obscene writer, Joyce thus unleashes his satirical weaponry against the enemies of *Ulysses*, freely adapting his text to the trials it is already undergoing in the courts and in the hands of hostile readers. I offer this as a minor but instructive example of how literary modernism could actually take form in response to conventional reading practice, wagering on its own capacity to provoke new counterpractices in reading.

However, a detail of Mrs. Bellingham's testimony suggests that Bloom's letters have a distinctive formal characteristic quite apart from their obscene content: they are written in several handwritings and as such are roughly analogous to the form of *Ulysses*, itself written in several styles. In an obscene letter, such a tactic would presumably serve to conceal the writer's identity, whereas Joyce's several styles have a more defensible aesthetic purpose. The effect of Joyce's trial scene, however, is to make the very heterogeneity of the text part of the offense committed against bourgeois readerly expectations, and in this way he fires a preemptive shot against anticipated readings of *Ulysses*.

Apart from the activity of his writing in itself, Joyce did more than most writers to prepare for a favorable reception of his work in those quarters that he accurately judged to be most powerful in ensuring its critical and commercial success. It is difficult to think of any other writer who could organize a scholarly symposium on his own *Work in Progress,* assign topics to the assembled experts, and publish the results, complete with a "letter of protest" written by himself under an assumed name (see Beckett 1962). However, it is doubtful that even Joyce could have anticipated the extent to which *Ulysses* took on a life of its own in the world outside the text. Since its publication in 1922, the fate of *Ulysses* testifies to a range of readings and other uses beyond not only the author's control but also beyond the control of any authority that might conceivably be exercised by the text itself.

Ulysses is not just a book. It is one of those cultural icons of the kind defined by Roland Barthes that can be emptied of one set of meanings and filled with another according to the forces of economics and ideology. As such, it has been variously personified in the discourses of the media and of literary criticism, where it has suffered a series of misadventures comparable in their rigor to those of Bloom himself: thus one has seen trials of *Ulysses* and scandals of *Ulysses.* The recent publication of a so-called "reader's edition" has been described in the *Times Literary Supplement* by Stephen Joyce, the author's grandson, as "the rape of *Ulysses*" (June 27, 1997).

What the *Times Literary Supplement* has sensationally called "The Real Scandal of *Ulysses*" (January 31, 1997) concerns the manner in which Shakespeare and Co.'s original edition of the novel was sold in a limited "deluxe" edition of one thousand copies offered in large part to dealers who in turn sold to collectors, making the novel inaccessible in a real sense to readers of ordinary means. Based on the publicity the book had garnered mainly through the obscenity trials, Joyce and his publishers accurately predicted that copies of the first edition would rise substantially in value. Writing on this episode in publishing history, Lawrence Rainey argues that the strategy of offering *Ulysses* in a deluxe edition reconceived the idea of readership, transforming the reader into "a collector, an investor, or even a speculator" (1996, 539). The book had entered into an economy of value that had little to do with the practice of reading itself.

If we accept the thesis of a new heterogeneity of reading, two points can be made here about the transformation of the reading public that had taken place since the nineteenth century. The first is that the unified public addressed by Victorian writers had been segmented according to differing tastes, or by what Pierre Bourdieu would define as levels of cultural capital. Second, this segmentation was also marked by real economic difference, that is, by the uneven distribution of capital itself. The modernist movement was closely associated with this phenomenon, with perilous consequences for the fate of reading. As Rainey remarks, "the effect of modernism was not so much to encourage reading as to render it superfluous" (542).

If, quite apart from its artistic merits, *Ulysses* became the first wholly commodified novel, its integration in recent years into the economy of popular culture has transformed it into something that I propose to call a hypercommodity. By this I mean an object that not only has market value in itself, but that in addition to this serves as a vehicle for marketing other commodities, services, and institutions. One example is the use of Joyce's name and of *Ulysses* for marketing Jameson's Irish whiskey. Advertising in a special Bloomsday supplement to the *Irish Times* (June 16, 1998), the Jameson distillery exploits Joyce's own supposed preference for this drink and points out the coincidence that Joyce's initials are also those of the distiller John Jameson. Allusions to the whiskey are quoted from *Ulysses* and *Finnegans Wake*. Finally, Jameson's announces its sponsorship of a series of public readings of *Ulysses* to take place around the world on Bloomsday:

> Beginning with Chapter One in Melbourne at 8 a.m. Irish time, the reading moves westward through 18 cities, including Tokyo, Trieste, Paris, London, Dublin, and New York. An extract from each of the 18 chapters is being read in each city.

In this truly postmodern event, a simulacrum of reading takes place, fragmented in space and time on a global scale, and orchestrated by the corporate planning skills of international business. One could hardly wish for a better demonstration of the coincidence of modernist literary form, the dispersion of readership, and the globalization of markets.

Perhaps more remarkable from the political perspective is the extent to which the governments of Dublin Corporation and the Irish Republic, historically hostile to Joyce, have now adopted the author and *Ulysses* as symbols of the Irish capital, the Irish nation, and by extension their own legitimacy. Among those participating in Jameson's worldwide reading of *Ulysses* was Mary McAleese, president of the Republic of Ireland. Joyce's portrait now appears on the Irish ten-pound note, with a tribute to Anna Livia Plurabelle, the heroine of *Finnegans Wake*, on the verso face. In Dublin, *Ulysses* is used heavily as a vehicle for promoting tourism in the city, with tourist materials recommending pubs and pointing out other locations mentioned in the novel. Amid the euphoria, it is not mentioned that Joyce could not publish his work in Ireland; that *Ulysses* contains scathing critiques of Irish nationalism as well as of British imperialism; that Joyce refused to visit his native country after the Civil War of 1922–23; that he never accepted the principle of partition; and that he held on to his British passport rather than accept citizenship from the truncated Irish Free State.

When any practice becomes sufficiently heterogeneous, it reaches a point of self-annihilation, that is, a point at which the various forms of the practice have less in common with one another than with any number of other practices. The fate of reading appears to have reached this point, where it disappears into the accelerated time and space of modernity, there to merge with the variegated and fragmentary impulses of perception itself. Joyce understood this and saw that the form of "reading" most adapted to the contemporary environment is the instantaneous and mostly unconscious apprehension of advertisement. So it is that Bloom's "final meditations" have a prophetic character. They are of an ideal text consisting of

> some one sole unique advertisement to cause passers to stop in wonder, a poster novelty, . . . reduced to its simplest and most efficient terms not exceeding the span of casual vision and congruous with the velocity of modern life. (*U* 17.1770–73)

Yet in the midst of the bewildering universe of texts evoked in his work, Joyce still imagines an ideal reader and his scene of reading. In *Ulysses* this scene occurs at the end of "Circe," when Bloom has a vision of his son Rudy, who died at the age of eleven days. Rudy now appears as "a fairy boy" of eleven years, the age he would be now if he had survived. He is dressed in an Eton suit with glass shoes and a little bronze helmet. He holds a book in his hand and *"reads from right to left inaudibly, smiling, kissing the page"* (*U* 15.4959). The image suggests a young Jewish scholar reading a sacred text in Hebrew, but it is also Joyce's figure of the ideal reader in his innocent *jouissance,* one for whom the pleasure of the text is the fulfillment of desire. His reading from right to left implies not only a sacred text but also a reading back to origins, an orthographic figure for a Proustian recovery of the past. In Joyce this movement of return has its own historical dimension, taking us back to Hellenic as well as Judeo-Christian origins. So it is that Rudy, with his bronze helmet and slim ivory cane, recalls the figure of Hermes with his helmet and staff. Hermes is a god of arts, the inventor of the lyre, and, as one who deals in dreams, a suitable figure for the end of this oniric sequence. As messenger of the gods, he is also the original interpreter of the divine and thus an ideal figure for reading as a hermeneutic. It is as if, for the culminating scene of a visionary text, Joyce had his own vision of the perfect reader and text, both created by him, meant wholly for each other, and meeting finally in an afterlife.

The figure of an ideal reader resurfaces in Joyce's last work, *Finnegans Wake,* in an episode devoted to the examination of a manuscript that looks suspiciously like the *Wake* itself. We are told that this work is "sentenced to be nuzzled over a full trillion times for ever and a night till his noddle sink or swim by the ideal reader suffering from an ideal insomnia" (*FW* 120.12–14). *Finnegans Wake* is a night book, where language is fragmented according to the logic of dreams, as if written in anticipation of Lacan's theory that the unconsciousness is structured like a language. The ideal reader of such a work enters a world whose reality is ordinarily accessible only through the portals of sleep, but he enters it awake and hears the voice of the unconscious with a full if bewildered consciousness. His insomnia is ideal not because it prevents him from sleeping, but because it allows him to explore the world of sleep without surrendering the interpretive power that sleep ordinarily takes from us. Seen in this light, Joyce's ideal reader looks, after all, very much like Proust's, who is able to receive communication from another without surrendering the intellectual autonomy enjoyed in solitude. Joyce's formula implicitly replaces "the other" in Proust with the unconscious, but it comes to the same thing, the unconscious being other by definition.

In the original story of Ulysses, the god Hermes gives Odysseus an herb called *moly* that allows him to enjoy the charms of Circe without being turned, like his men, into swine. So it is with the ideal reader in both Proust and Joyce, who is given a kind of talismanic protection against the spell of the text, enabling him to experience its otherness without sacrificing his own freedom.

6

Fatal Signatures

Forgery and Colonization in *Finnegans Wake*

Forgeries real and imagined form a recurring motif throughout Joyce's later work. In *Ulysses* Stephen recalls the forged letter with which Hamlet sends Rosencrantz and Guildenstern to their deaths; Bloom speculates on forgeries of Holy Writ and of *Hamlet* itself. *Finnegans Wake* turns repeatedly to Richard Pigott's forged letters, designed to implicate Charles Stewart Parnell in the Phoenix Park murders of 1882. And behind all this, as a kind of primal scene of forgery, the *Wake* continually reenacts Jacob's usurpation of his brother's birthright, where Jacob's kid gloves forge the "signature" of Esau's hairy hands.

The particular form of transgression represented by forgery allows for its elaboration in *Finnegans Wake* on three levels: as an instrument of colonization, as a figure for the nature of writing, and as a metaphor for artistic creation. Joyce's interest in forgery and in the scenes of violence and oppression surrounding it derive from what Derrida calls the violence of the letter. Derrida uses this phrase specifically in connection with colonizing activity, as in the case of Levi-Strauss's "writing lesson" administered to the Nambikwara of Brazil, even when such activity is not practiced under the "actual banner of colonial oppression" (1976, 107). In a larger sense, forgery for Derrida is the unveiled character of writing itself as a gesture of displacement and usurpation whose conditions of possibility are those of absence, and, ultimately, death (1991). However, in a paradox that Joyce is happy to exploit, forgery also stands synecdochically for writing in a creative sense: writing is precisely that which is forged, wrought out of crude matter, like the conscience of his race that Stephen goes forth to create in *A Portrait of the Artist as a Young Man*.

In the vast terrain of cultural memory traversed by the *Wake*, the associations of forgery with colonization, writing, and art are more than just alternate levels of signification; they are signs that penetrate and contaminate one another, just as the forge of artistic creation is never entirely pure of the offense of forgery. Joyce's work erases the boundary between forgery and forging, between writing as violence and writing as fabulous artifice; in the binding work of the forge, the boundary becomes "innate little bondery" (*FW* 296.34)

I propose to explore this paradox through an investigation of two figures, or gestures, that Joyce associates closely with forgery: (1) *hesitency,* the misspelled word that exposed Pigott's forgeries in the Special Commission hearings of 1888–89 and that recurs throughout the *Wake,* and (2) the *signature,* which has what Derrida calls a "divided agency," testifying both to the absence and the mysterious presence of the signatory. Joyce's treatment of the signature—and of the hesitancy that often accompanies acts of writing and signing—has consequences not just for a theory of colonization through literal and figurative forgeries but also for a feminist perspective on this aspect of Joyce's work. As the condition for the establishment of patriarchal as well as colonial authority, forgery is the crime of writing concealed in the Name of the Father, the fraudulent origin of the Father's privilege as divinely or naturally conferred.

*   *   *

The hearings of the Special Commission on Charges and Allegations of 1888–89 hold a storied place in the memory of Irish colonization; in what they afforded both of tragedy and farce, they also form an important part of the background to *Finnegans Wake.* Students of Irish history will recall the main elements of the story: the inflammatory *Times* series of 1887 on "Parnellism and Crime"; the letters linking Parnell to the Phoenix Park assassinations; the formation of the Special Commission; the sensational exposure of Pigott's forgeries; and his flight to Madrid, where he blew his brains out in a room at the Hotel Embajadores.

The entire affair is a classic case of alliance between the press and the government in enforcing colonial rule. The incriminating letters helped to gain passage of the Coercion Bill of 1887, which gave the government sweeping new powers against the nationalist campaign, including summary prosecution of offenses such as boycotting, intimidation, conspiracy against rent, resistance to eviction, and unlawful assembly (Lyons 378). The role of the *Times,* however, has an element of journalistic self-destruction. Having published the first of these letters with assurances that its authenticity had been established "by a process the accuracy of which cannot be impugned" (April 18, 1887), the *Times* went on to record on a daily basis the complete transcripts of the proceedings by which its authenticity—and that of the letters published subsequently—was demolished.

Apart from their political and symbolic significance, the hearings offered a model for certain rhetorical situations in the *Wake*. Both the *Times* series and the actual hearings involved detailed physical examination of the letters of the kind that is parodied in the *Wake*. In reproducing the infamous "facsimile" letter, purported to be Parnell's apology to Patrick Egan for having publicly denounced the Phoenix Park assassinations, the *Times* reports having subjected this document to "a most careful and minute scrutiny" and notes not only the handwriting and signature but also the quality of the paper ("an ordinary sheet of stout white notepaper") and an erasure in the manuscript as "undesigned evidence of authenticity" (April 18, 1887). In *Finnegans Wake* the letter of I.5 is examined with no less scrutiny and with a similar tone of accusation. Written on "a goodish sized sheet of letterpaper" (*FW* 111.9), it bears teastains and other "accretions of terricious matter" (*FW* 114.28–29), as well as "numerous stabs and gashes made by a pronged instrument" (*FW* 124.2–3) later determined to be a fork. The handwriting is "the fatal droopanddwindle slope of a blamed scrawl, a sure sign of imperfectible moral blindness" (*FW* 122.34–36). It is, in other words, an authentic document written with base motives, precisely the imputation made by the *Times* concerning the facsimile letter signed with the name of Parnell.

The hearings as recorded in the *Times* provide an equally compelling paradigm for the rhetorical mode of cross-examination. Sir Charles Russell's relentless interrogation of Pigott prefigures the inquisition of Shaun in *FW* III.3, who is questioned on his association with a certain "counterfeit Kevin": "Now, have you reasonable hesitancy in your mind about him after fourpriest redmass or are you in your post? Tell me andat sans dismay" (*FW* 483.12–13). Shaun's postal activities, like his role as recalcitrant witness, link him to Pigott, deliverer of the counterfeit letters to the *Times*. Pigott is also allied to Shem, however, in his character as a sham—a destitute and shiftless inventor of fictions.

Russell's cross-examination reached its climax in questioning Pigott on the letter dated January 9, 1882—four months before the Phoenix Park murders—which had Parnell upbraiding his associates for their inaction: "What are these fellows waiting for? . . . Let there be an end to this hesitency." Russell, having asked Pigott to write the word "hesitancy" in court, noted that Pigott had misspelled it with an "e," just as it was mis-spelled in the letter. Pigott's lame, self-contradicting explanations drew only laughter from the gallery (*Times*, February 22, 1889). The next day Pigott confessed to the forgeries, then, still hesitant, partly recanted before fleeing the country. So HCE, fleeing the scene of his own trial at the end of *FW* I.4, is undone by "the spoil of hesitants, the spell of hesitency" (*FW* 97.25). The fatal "spell of hesitency" connects both Pigott and HCE to that tragic forger and figure of guilt, Hamlet, described in *Ulysses* as "a hesitat-ing soul . . . torn by conflicting doubts, as one sees in real life" (*U* 9.3–4). Thus the disgrace and flight of Pigott are incorporated into the *Wake's* general symptomatology of guilt, where HCE's discourse of "HeCitEncy!" (*FW* 421.19) is marked by contradictory, self-incriminating apologies spo-ken in a "doubling stutter" (*FW* 197.5).

Stephen Heath has noted the role of forgery in what he calls the *Wake's* "strategies of hesitation," or the constant destabilization and displacement of meaning through the misappropriation of other texts. For Heath, the *Wake's* radical "discontinuity in progress" produces a "profound and ir-reparable fragmentation" that breaks free from context into a dehisto-ricized space of intertextuality: "Joyce's texts . . . in their unstabilization, their 'hecitency,' refer not to a context—and thus not to a 'Reality' . . . but to an intertext" (39).

While acknowledging Heath's contribution to an understanding of the *Wake's* structural relation to other texts, my own approach insists on a historical context for these same strategies; far from destroying its context, the *Wake* remains deeply imbedded in the ambiguities of modernity and the (post)colonial condition. Rather than destabilizing a historical context that would be in itself coherent, stable, and intelligible, Joyce's writing re-flects a historical context that is always already destabilized, itself a "dis-continuity in progress." When one of the inquisitors says in the cross-examination of *FW* III.3, "Language this allsfare for the loathe of Marses ambiviolent about it" (*FW* 518.2–3), he signals the ambivalent relation, in language, of love to loathing, of Moses, deliverer from oppression, to Mars, god of war; this "ambiviolence" applies not only to Joyce's text but also to the world in which it is written. Thus colonial violence is not simply the colonizer's oppression of the colonized; it is also an "ambiviolence" in which guilt and innocence, oppression and liberation, authenticity and forgery are profoundly mixed.

The same ambivalence marks the historical context in which forgery is used as an instrument of colonial domination. From the perspective of anticolonial resistance, such methods conform to a logic in which the colonizing enterprise is itself a form of forgery. Colonization has been compared to writing, as the trace, the mark of possession, the appropriation of the pure space of the page, creating a hierarchy of signification that opposes the body of the text to its margins. The idea of colonization as forgery merely strengthens this metaphor, since the ideology of colonial domination is writing in the name of another, passing oneself off as someone else, one's motives as nobler than they are; such acts as appropriation, annexation, and relegation of the colonized to the margins of the cultural order are performed in the name of union, civilization, and empire. Conrad's Marlow, on being named "an emissary of light," describes "a queer feeling . . . that I was an impostor. Odd thing that I . . . had a moment—I won't say of hesitation, but of startled pause, before this commonplace affair" (76–77). Against the imposture and forgery of the colonizer, the politics of resistance posits the authenticity of the colonized as an indigenous people, the most authentic being those who, like Lévi-Strauss's Nambikwara, are altogether innocent of writing.

Joyce, however, resists the simple analogy that holds that colonizer is to colonized as forgery is to authenticity. Instead, he exposes the elements of hybridity, complicity, and internal contradiction marking these apparent oppositions. The pathetic, impoverished Pigott is about as likely a figure of colonial domination as the magisterial Parnell is a victim of oppression. So the figure of HCE, alternately blustering and beleaguered, swaggering and staggering, denies the familiar opposition of oppressor and victim. Fleeing the scene of his trial in I.4, HCE is linked to Pigott, as we have seen, by "the spell of hesitency," but the exclamatory remark, "Reynard is slow!" (*FW* 97.28) links him to Parnell as well. For if Pigott forged the name of Parnell, Parnell committed his own forgery, passing by the name of "Mr. Fox," among other aliases, in his adulterous liaison with Katherine O'Shea.

The dialogue of Mutt and Jute in I.1 dramatizes the shared guilt and hesitancy of colonizer and colonized. Advised by Jute, the perennial invader, to "become a bitskin more wiseable," the native Mutt replies:

Has? Has at? Hasatency? Urp Boohooru! Booru Usurp! I trumple from rath in mine mines when I rimimirim! (*FW* 16.26–28)

On one level this is a cry of defiance, echoing the Swahili call for liberation—"Uhuru!"—and the war cry of the mutinous Hindu sepoy "waxing ranjymad" against Wellington in the Willingdone Museyroom: "Ap Pukskaru! Pukka Yurap!" (*FW* 10.17). Trembling with the wrath of the oppressed, Mutt remembers the glory of Brian Boru, the High King of Ireland who defeated the Norse invaders at Clontarf in 1014. This wrath, however, is stunned by the "surd" of stupidity and thwarted by the hesitancy of a stammer: "Has? Has at? Hasatency?" It is soon quieted, in any case, by the bribe of the invader, who, proposing that bygones be bygones, greases his palm with a gilt trinket: "Bisons is bisons. Let me fore all your hasitancy cross your qualm with trink gilt" (*FW* 16.29–30). Mutt responds with the traditional Irish welcome (*céad míle fáilte*) and invites the invader to have a look around the island: "Cead mealy faulty rices for one dabblin bar" (*FW* 16.34–35). In the transfer of gilt from Jute to Mutt, the guilt of the colonizer is transferred to the colonized subject, now guilty of collaborating with the invader; his hesitant stammer in remembering the resistance of Brian Boru is a symptom of that guilt.

As if to emphasize this state of ambivalence uniting colonizer with colonized, HCE's mythic prototype, Finn MacCool, is described in I.6 as "unhesitant in his unionism and yet a pigotted nationalist" (*FW* 133.14–15). A pigotted nationalist is among other things a bigoted one, like Michael Cusack, founder of the Gaelic Athletic Association in 1884 and the model for the Citizen in *Ulysses,* whose ultranationalism rises to a pitch of xenophobic hysteria. Joyce's phrase also reminds us of Richard Pigott's career as an Irish nationalist: an activist in the early Home Rule movement and a sworn member of the Irish Republican Brotherhood, he published three nationalist newspapers later bought by Parnell (Ervine 177). A "pigotted nationalist," then, would be both an extremist, like the Citizen, and a traitor, like Pigott, a combination which suggests the violent instability of nationalist feeling as well as its affinity with unhesitant, or bigoted, unionism.

On HCE's own back door has been nailed "an inkedup name and title, inscribed in the national cursives, accelerated, regressive, filiform, turreted and envenomoloped in piggotry" (*FW* 99.17–19). In this description bigotry joins forgery—the cooked up, inkedup name and title—to Irish writing as the "national cursives," recalling the historical connection between nationalist violence and the revival of the Irish language, as both were advocated by leaders of the Young Ireland movement such as the poets Thomas Davis and John Edward Pigot (O'Hegarty 613). For Joyce, then, the real violence of nationalism and colonialism can be traced to the symbolic violence imposed by the letter; to act *à la lettre* (according to the letter), is to obey the law, to submit to its threat of violence. How, then, does one write without merely perpetuating this institutional inscription of violence? Joyce's solution is both pacifist and anarchist: the "abnihili-sation of the eytm" (*FW* 353.22), the sabotage of the letter enacted in *Finnegans Wake*.

*   *   *

Strictly speaking, the notion of forgery presupposes not just writing but specifically the signature—the trace of the writer, the sign of the writer's difference from others, a supplement nonetheless integral to the text, a mark of property, of the text as proper to that writer. As Derrida has shown, however, the signature also functions as a kind of epitaph. The fi-nality and materiality of the signature reflects a certain fatality. In the act of signing, the signatory makes provision for his or her own absence and even death, as the laws of probate make clear. Here are ample grounds for hesitancy. But not to sign is to relinquish authority and even not to exist in a certain legal sense. In a very concrete way, then, the signature both af-firms one's presence and creates the conditions for one's absence: we live and die not by the sword but by the pen.

Among the several passages where forgery, forging, hesitancy, and the signature are brought together is one of the Night Lessons of *FW* II.2, where a voice I take to be Shaun's says to Shem: "And that salubrated sickenagiaour of yaours have teaspilled all my hazeydency. Forge away, Sunny Sim!" (*FW* 305.3–5). Here the celebrated signature is both salubri-ous and sickening; that is, it is the sign and cause of the signatory's life and death, recalling Plato's critique of writing as the ambivalent *pharmakon:* both poison and remedy for the *logos* of memory. According to the *Phae-drus*, writing serves as an aid to memory but also weakens the original power of memory by displacing its function as well as its contents, the *logos*, onto an artificial *teknè*. Memory thus constitutes an origin and mas-tery of the *logos* that is threatened by the invention of writing.

It is here that a perspective relevant to feminist concerns opens on the subject of writing and the signature, for Derrida shows Plato's myth to be an allegory for patriarchal authority (1991, 124–37). In the myth, the *logos* as truth and law is closely identified with paternal origin and authority. (Here we might compare the Egyptian myth of Theuth, which Plato cites, to the first verse of the Gospel of John: "In the beginning was the *logos*, and the *logos* was with God, and the *logos* was God.") Joyce dramatizes the awesome word of the Father at the end of the "Children's Hour" chapter (II.1), where "the Clearer of the Air from on high has spoken," terrifying the "unhappitents of the earth" into submission and prayer (*FW* 258.20–22. Compare Derrida 1984; 1987, 15–53).

Now when writing usurps the univocal authority of the Father, it performs a double function: on one hand, like a clever son it mimics the Father's word and name and so pretends to an authority it does not possess in an originary sense. On the other hand, it subverts that authority in its quality as pure repetition without proper identity or substance (1991, 122). This is exactly what happens at the end of the "Children's Hour." Joyce's language and imagery here follow the Book of Exodus, where the Word of the Father is rendered into writing for the first time as a supplement and an aid to memory. By giving instructions for his altar to be built, God says, "I cause my name to be remembered" (Exod. 20.24), and likewise he writes his commandments so that Moses may teach them (Exod. 24.12). In the same spirit of faith in the written word, a pious voice in the *Wake* prays "that thy children may read in the book of the opening of the mind to light" (*FW* 258.31–32). Joyce thus evokes the scriptural tradition of the Book as the material but uncorrupted form of the Word of the Father.

The Platonic and biblical traditions are alike in locating the purity and origin of the *logos* in the Father's Word; they differ, however, in the matter of what happens to the *logos* when it is written down. The Bible remains the Word of God; but for Plato any form of writing carries the danger of corruption and unauthorized dissemination. For Joyce as well, the written inscription of the *logos* makes possible the mimicry of prayer and the subversive laughter of human art with which the "Children's Hour" ends: "Loud, heap miseries upon us yet entwine our arts with laughters low" (*FW* 259.7–8).

Where Joyce departs from both the Platonic and the biblical traditions, however, is in his interpretation of the "original" word of the Father, which he sees or hears as *already* forged, artificially amplified or "moguphonoised" (*FW* 258.21–22), an act of grandiloquent ventriloquism, like the voice of the Wizard of Oz whose fraudulence is discovered by Dorothy. There is little evidence that Joyce knew L. Frank Baum's children's story of 1900, but his book can similarly be read as a parable of the daughter's liberation from the oppressive word of the Father. Joyce's text thus serves as fertile ground for Derrida's theory that the subversive character and essential forgery that Platonic tradition ascribes to writing applies no less to the paternal *logos*, and that the myth of writing as corruption and supplement is in fact designed to establish through opposition the idea of original authority and purity in the Father's word.

According to this theory, writing is a highly ambivalent instrument whose mimicry of the Father can be used either to reinforce the structures of patriarchal power or to expose the forged origins of such structures. In this latter sense, writing is a friend to subversion and to the cause of liberation from the totalizing symbolic order of patriarchy. It seems clear to me that Joyce is committed to writing in this sense, and that this is where his project prefigures the forms of feminism that have developed in association with poststructuralist criticism.

Joyce's writing in fact both reproduces and parodies its own ambivalent relation to male systems of authority. The letter of FW I.5 may be seen as a synecdoche for the *Wake* in its embodiment of an erotic struggle between a male and a female written hand:

> the penelopean patience of its last paraphe, a colophon of no fewer
> than seven hundred and thirtytwo strokes tailed by a leaping lasso—
> who thus at all marvelling will but press on hotly to see the vaulting
> feminine libido of those interbranching ogham sex upinandinsweeps
> sternly controlled and easily repersuaded by the uniform matterof-
> factness of a meandering male fist? (*FW* 123.4–10)

Here the letter is compared most directly to the "Penelope" episode of *Ulysses*, which completes the 732 pages of the book's first edition in an act of authorial cross-dressing: Joyce writing in a woman's hand, forging the female signature. However, the language of excess both in the passage quoted above and in the lines immediately preceding it—"the toomuchness, the fartoomanyness of all those fourlegged ems" (*FW* 122.36–123.1)—suggests an analogy with the *Wake* itself in its qualities of overflow, abundant superfluity, and inexhaustible possibility: the *Wake*, in other words, as the textual embodiment of feminine excess as *jouissance*, that which extends "beyond the phallus" and exceeds the grasp of the symbolic order constructed in the name of the Father (Lacan 1982, 145). The particular pleasures of this text are driven by what may be described, for its all-embracing and infinitely connected abundance, as a feminine libido that is hardly controlled by a uniform male matter-of-factness.

Joyce's parodies of such male authority form an essential comic element of his text, as in the mock scholarship cited later on page 123: "v. *Some Forestallings over that Studium of Sexophonologistic Schizophrenisis*, vol. xxiv, pp. 2–555" (*FW* 123.17–19). We should not fail to notice, however, that the title of Professor Duff-Muggli's paper neatly addresses Joyce's own concerns with phonologism, or the conventional primacy of speech over writing; with the problem of sexual identity in writing; and with the schizoid nature of writing as it uneasily combines male and female elements. This *studium*, conceivably another metonym for the *Wake* itself, is naturally pursued with considerable forestalling, that is, hesitancy.

The very nature of the letter's "last paraphe" implies the struggle that Joyce evokes between feminine libido and male repression in writing. The *Oxford English Dictionary* defines a paraph as "a flourish made after a signature, originally as a kind of precaution against forgery." The character of the paraph as a flourish—that is, an extravagant gesture lavished on the economy of the signature—runs counter to its function as a security measure against forgery. The paraph is then both a figure of desire and an instrument of prohibition, reproducing in this double character the creative as well the limiting capacities of writing: writing as desire, resistance, liberation; writing as prohibition, colonization, the law of the Father.

As the act of writing that registers the affirmation of the signatory, the signature betrays another ambiguity: on one hand, it establishes a person's identity as authentic; on the other hand, it exposes the fact that, for legal as well as other purposes, such authenticity resides only in writing. The signature's relation to some a priori authenticity is a matter of faith and, ultimately, a fiction sustained only by convention. To refuse or to be unable to sign one's name is, in a sense, to cease to exist. But to sign is also to *consign* oneself to writing, to relinquish one's "authentic" identity to the authority of signs embodied in writing. Stephen's hesitancy and ultimate refusal to sign MacCann's petition for universal peace (*P* 196–98) is thus both an attempt to preserve his identity as an artist (which must itself be "forged" in the double sense) and a refusal to commit the forgery of signing a document that does not represent his convictions and that he finds suspect in its origins and motives. Stephen considers the Czar's photograph, designed to authenticate the petition, to be an idolatrous icon, a bogus substitute for "a legitimate Jesus" (*P* 198). By withholding his signature Stephen seeks to create its value; his own legitimacy as "a priest of the eternal imagination" (*P* 221) can only be established, *forged*, through opposition to an illegitimate savior. The irony, of course, is that this authenticity does not exist in its own right; it is created only by the designation of the inauthentic.

In the "Night Lessons" passage from the *Wake* cited above, Shaun claims that Shem's signature has "teaspilled all my hazeydency" (*FW* 305.4), dispelled all his hesitancy. But as we have seen both in Derrida and in the episode of the petition in *Portrait*, the action of the signature as a remedy in dispelling the reader's hesitancy serves only to reintroduce the poison of forgery. This contamination of the signature by hesitation and forgery is suggested by the marginal annotation (*FW* 305) where Shem's "stuttering hand" translates into a fantastic blend of Italian and Latin the question put by Sir Charles Russell to Pigott in the witness box at the Law Courts: "COME SI COMPITA CUNCTITITITILATIO?" "How do you spell hesitatatatancy?"

*   *   *

Apart from being the sign of Pigott's forgery, *hesitency* also stands for the hesitation before any act whose fatal consequence, in Hamlet's words, "must give us pause" (3.1.68). Pigott's forgeries were in fact his death warrant, leading to his suicide. But as Derrida reminds us, all writing must give us pause for the way it functions in the radical absence of any given writer or reader: "It is a break in presence, 'death,' or the possibility of the 'death' of the addressee [or sender], inscribed in the structure of the mark" (1991, 91). There is, then, a gap or a rupture that divides the writer from his or her writing, even from that writer's signature, a parting recognized in the poetic convention of the *envoi*. Joyce acknowledges as much in the final line of *Giacomo Joyce:* "Envoy: Love me, love my umbrella" (16). My umbrella, *mon ombre là*, my shadow there: writing in its character as envoy casts the shadow of death over the writer. When Shem writes, "I'm only out for celebridging the guilt of the gap in your hiscitendency" (*FW* 305.8–9), he acknowledges the *aporia* in the act of writing, the doubt we experience as our writing is orphaned and cast adrift in an iterability that already outlives us.

Yet writing, in creating this gap, also bridges over it by celebrating, "celebridging," its infinite ability to recreate the subject, to free him or her from the paralysis of guilt, just as Freud's "talking cure" is designed to do: to construct the story of a coherent self over the paralyzing chasm of guilt. Writing simultaneously testifies to the void and throws a bridge over it, and this is precisely the paradox celebrated by Joyce's work. As implied in the "salubrated sickenagiaour," this celebration is closely related to the function of the signature. Derrida compares the characteristic mode of affirmation in Joyce's later work—the "yes" of Joyce—to the mode of affirmation enacted by the act of signing; to sign is to affirm, to say yes. As Derrida points out, however, the signature is always a countersignature, a copy supposed to conform to some original that in fact does not exist: in

other words, it is a kind of forgery. The signature is not authentic in itself
but derives value from its relation to other instances of the signature before and after, just as the word "yes" has meaning only as part of a series in
which each instance of affirmation says "yes" to the preceding one. In publishing the facsimile letter, the *Times* invites members of Parliament to
verify its authenticity for themselves:

> If any member of Parliament doubts the fact, he can easily satisfy
> himself on the matter by comparing the handwriting with that of Mr.
> Parnell in the book containing the signatures of members when they
> first take their seats in the House of Commons. (April 18, 1887)

We may compare the *Times*'s "satisfaction" to Joyce's celebration, both
testifying to the manner in which the repetition of the signature represents the triumph of affirmation over doubt. The difference is that where
the *Times* celebrates a false authenticity, Joyce celebrates his liberation
from what is for the artist a bogus distinction between authentic and inauthentic. Derrida's analogy is to an infinite structure of parody in which
each parodic gesture is parodied in turn (1987, 89–101). Such is the case
with Joyce's own celebrated signature, *Finnegans Wake*, where parody, affirmation, and laughter are forged through the generation of this synthetic system, erected like a fragile bridge over the gap of the blank page.
The text is related to its historical context, then, not as to an origin but as to
a preceding set of terms in the series perpetuated by the text. In returning
to this context, I will show how Joyce's treatment of forgery and its companion crime, plagiarism, questions within the value of the signature itself
the notions of origin, authenticity, and ownership being contested in the
political arena defined by colonialism.

Plagiarism is forgery's mirror image: where the plagiarist signs his or
her own name to another's writing, the forger signs another's name to his
or her own writing. Both of these crimes of the letter undermine the conventions of origin and ownership linking author to text, and that is what
makes them paradigms for the subversive strategies of *Finnegans Wake*. In
I.7 Shaun remarks of Shem:

> What do you think Vulgariano did but study with stolen fruit how
> cutely to copy all their various styles of signature so as one day to
> utter an epical forged cheque on the public for his own private profit.
> (*FW* 181.16–19)

Who can say how many pseudostylic shamiana, how few or how many of the most venerated public impostures, how very many piously forged palimpsests slipped in the first place by this morbid process from his pelagiarist pen? (*FW* 181.36–182.3)

"Pelagiarist" combines plagiarism with the Pelagian heresy—which denied the doctrine of Original Sin—and with the Greek *pelagios* (of the sea). The image is one of both unlimited freedom—cashing a monumental check, escaping one's origins, voyaging on the open sea—and complete entanglement in the black market of stolen textual goods implied by the crimes of forgery and plagiarism. This vision of intertextuality renders irrelevant ideas of textual origin, authorship, and authenticity, while it also ties writing to the textual field—the context—from which, scrap by scrap, it is purloined.

This perspective would appear to demystify the signature and expose it as a sham, an "inked up name and title" out of the cache of stolen merchandise from which other forms of writing are produced. Returning to the examination of ALP's letter in I.5, we find the question of the signature raised explicitly by the Shaunlike voice that conducts the inquiry: "So why, pray, sign anything as long as every word, letter, penstroke, paperspace is a perfect signature of its own?" (*FW* 115.6–8). This person argues for the superfluity of the signature as such, only to reinstate the signature at a deeper level of personal identity. The signature is not needed because it is always already there: the author is known by his or her style or personal touch, just as we recognize a friend by "his personal touch, habits of full or undress, movements, response to appeals for charity" (*FW* 115.9–10) and so forth. Thus one does away with the signature as such only to make everything signature. This confident affirmation of the authenticity of personal identity, however, is rendered suspect in part because of the speaker to whom it is attributed, one who professes his faith in public order, the police, and talking "straight turkey" (*FW* 113.23–26). A tombstone mason (*FW* 113.34) dedicated to raising monuments to the dead, he is contemptuous of the Shemlike person he addresses as a "poorjoist," a poor means of support, a perjurist, poor Joyce, whose *Portrait* is "just a poor trait of the artless" (*FW* 114.32). To put the defense of an inalienable and always readable personal identity or signature in the hands of such an advocate is to sabotage the idea from the start. It serves only to weaken further what should now be seen as the dubious conceptual opposition between forgery and authenticity.

In an essay on the "Eumaeus" chapter of *Ulysses,* Mark Osteen reads Joyce's allusions to various forged texts and identities in terms of an analogy between narrative fiction and counterfeit currency. Just as the idea of mimesis in fiction depends on a notion of truth as that which is imitated, the idea of the counterfeit "remains parasitical upon the existence (or the faith in the existence) of that which it 'counters'—something not counterfeit" (832). Logically, the notion of forgery depends on that of authenticity. But if this distinction collapses, then everything is equally both forged and authentic. Osteen suggests that the narrator of "Eumaeus," often identified as Bloom, is rather a counterfeit or forgery of Bloom, but that Bloom himself, a protean and often fraudulent figure, has no single identity on which a conventional forgery could be based. The result is a "collective intertextuality that subverts laws of literary originality and ownership" (837), as in the phrase "genuine forgeries" (*U* 16.781).

The case of Richard Pigott, one of authentic forgery, shows how forgery and authenticity are not only complicit with one another but are in a certain sense the same. In order for the letters to be proven forgeries, they must be proven authentic; that is, the authentic work of the forger must bear his unmistakable signature in the "fatal scrawl," the "sure sign" of his hand in the text itself. In Pigott's case, "the spell of hesitency" is both proof of forgery and his own authentic signature. In his letter, a document both of forged authenticity and authentic forgery, authenticity and forgery amount to the same thing. According to this example, authentic authorship is established by the particular stamp one places on one's forgery. The "forge" of the artist is the place where creation is faked and the fake is created, a highly original piece of fakery, aye "very like a whale's egg farced with pemmican" (*FW* 120.11), to cite Joyce's plagiarism of *Hamlet,* where Polonius, in a manner authentic to himself, fakes his agreement with Hamlet.

To say that the forged and the authentic are the same is to make one of those statements that are invariably cited by conservative critics in order to demonstrate the folly of poststructuralist criticism. Let us consider, however, that the notion of authenticity is a human invention designed to confer privilege, protection, and value; as such it participates in the fictive constructions belonging more obviously to what we more commonly recognize as forgery. Authenticity, like authority, is conferred; the authority of the patriarch or colonizer and the authenticity of writing share a fictive status, in the original, Latin sense of something made.

The aptness of the ambivalent figure joining plagiarism, fakery, and forgery to authenticity becomes clear when we consider the nature of *Finnegans Wake* itself. On one hand, Joyce's distinctive mark is immediately recognizable on every page; every word, letter, pen stroke is a perfect signature of its own. On the other hand, no other work of Joyce's is so clearly a pastiche, a pell-mell assemblage of fragments forged and plagiarized from the cultural memory of Western Europe and beyond. Derrida has remarked on the *Wake*'s fusion of forgery and invention: "In the simulacrum of this *forgery*, in the ruse of the invented word, the greatest possible memory is stamped and smelted" (1984, 148–49).

Imperial power relies on the enforcement of distinctions: is it forged or authentic, is it literature or not, is it nationalist or unionist, is Parnell or Pigott guilty or innocent? But such distinctions are melted down and recast in the great forge of *Finnegans Wake*. With the breakdown of the opposition forgery/authenticity, questions concerning the nature of origin and authorship resist the either/or, us/them logic of nationalist and colonialist discourses. The nationalist believes in the unity of true citizens of authentic Irish origin. For the imperialist, Irish history begins in an authentic sense only with the *parousia* of civilization. By resisting this logic, Joyce solves the problem of how to write a revolutionary, decolonized text in the language of the colonizer. *Finnegans Wake* thus can be assigned neither to the literary tradition of the imperial power nor to the localized resistance of the colonial subject. Both forged *and* authentic, both English *and* foreign, it is neither imperialist (in ideology, in narrative form) *nor* nationalist in its anti-imperialism. Instead, it collapses these antinomies in an anarchic explosion of laughter. As Roland Barthes writes in *S/Z*, "This is in fact the function of writing: to make ridiculous, to annul the power (the intimidation) of one language over another, to dissolve any metalanguage as soon as it is constituted" (98). The subversive function of *Finnegans Wake* is thus closely allied to its comedic function; its celebration of comic freedom is made possible by its power to render ideology ridiculous.

7

Writing in the *Wake* of Empire

When Joyce began writing *Finnegans Wake* in 1922, the British Empire was already beginning to disintegrate. In India, Gandhi had begun the first of several *satyagraha* campaigns against British rule. In East Africa, more than two hundred men and women were killed by police in Nairobi during a March 1922 demonstration against the colonial government, sowing the seeds of a violent resistance movement. In Ireland, the establishment of the Irish Free State (1921) prepared for the independence of the twenty-six counties of the South. These cracks in the imperial edifice were to deepen during the seventeen years in which Joyce wrote the *Wake* in self-imposed exile from the first colony to break away from the modern British Empire.

Long considered either a purely formalist tour de force or a curiosity for linguists, myth critics, and source-hunters, Joyce's last work has recently begun to be read as being deeply involved in the political currents of the period between the wars and of early-twentieth-century European history in general.[1] In particular, the historical reality of decolonization became one of the conditions for Joyce's last work, which makes decolonization into a discursive as well as a historical event. To read Joyce as a decolonized writer is to recognize that his historical perspective on the final stages of the imperial era coincides with his creation of a text that calls into question, formally and thematically, the structures of power from which writing is inherited. It is also to begin the process of rethinking Joyce's place in the context of European modernism, especially insofar as modernism has been held to represent a privileged aesthetic domain of an imperialist European society. For if one aspect of modernism was to resolve the contradictions existing between the individual subject and the imperialist state, another aspect—and here one thinks of Beckett, Kafka, and the later Joyce—was to make manifest those contradictions in the subjective and objective conditions of modernity that persisted as latent and unresolved. Written in the spirit of this latter project, the *Wake* declares its independence from imperial structures of discourse in order to create a text that one may call, in terms that sometimes prove useful, both postmodern and postcolonial.

Following a formulation by the historian Arif Dirlik, the term *postcolonial* may be used to describe (*a*) the actual conditions in formerly colonial societies, (*b*) a global condition coming after the period of modern European colonialism, and (*c*) a discourse concerning these two kinds of conditions that is informed by the "epistemological and psychic orientations" that these conditions have produced (332). My treatment of *Finnegans Wake* as a postcolonial text makes reference to the first two of these meanings—a newly decolonized Ireland and a world in which colonial institutions are already seen to be outmoded—as background for reading the *Wake* in the context of the third, that is, as the production of an artistic discourse made possible by these newly emergent national and global realities. Where Dirlik argues that such a formulation makes postcolonial discourse indistinguishable from that of postmodernism, I find the category of the postcolonial useful in describing that aspect of postmodernism (including the *Wake*) which specifically addresses questions of colonial authority as a historical and epistemological reality.

Joyce's parodies of colonialism and of imperialism in general are matched in their satirical force only by his parodies of Irish nationalism, a double refusal characteristic of more recent postcolonial writers such as G. V. Desani and Salman Rushdie. There is by now a tradition of twentieth-century writers descended from Joyce who recognize that even in its oppositional stance, nationalism repeats imperialism's master narratives of universal development, paternal property, and racial purity (Lloyd 46). This ironic refusal of both nationalism and imperialism, however, is accompanied in Joyce by the affirmation of a language designed not simply to subvert the prevailing discourses of colonization but rather to open a space beyond the simple opposition of colonizer and colonized. This is especially true of *Finnegans Wake*, where the play of language breaks free from the formations of authority that—in the empire of letters—prescribe meaning in terms of narrative, syntactical logic, intelligibility, and so on. Joyce's technique accelerates the signifying effects of language into a vertiginous plurality in which the logic of colonization is dismantled, flung loose from its moorings, and cast adrift in the flow of the *Wake*.

In this chapter I examine how Joyce anticipates later developments in theory by interpreting the discourse of colonization as a sign of phallic authority, and more specifically as the expression of masculine sexual desire. Here I follow Colin MacCabe's suggestion that the disruptive and revolutionary form of Joyce's language is designed to draw attention to the relations of language, desire, and power, particularly as these are historically constructed in the forms of discourse, sexuality, and politics (133). Similar issues are raised in David Lloyd's suggestive study of Yeats, Beckett, and other Irish writers read in the context of "the postcolonial moment."

As Joyce writes it, "coglionial expancian" (*FW* 488.32) is formed out of two words in demotic Italian: *coglione* (stupid) and *coglioni* (testicles) (McHugh 1991); colonial expansion thus writes itself as the literal exposure, erection, and transgression of the male sex. The famous episode in which an Irish soldier named Buckley shoots a Russian general (II.3) takes place against the background of the Crimean War, that great clash of nineteenth-century Western and Eastern empires, "where obelisk rises when odalisks fall" (*FW* 335.33). The conquest of the odalisque—the languid Oriental harem girl—inspires the erection of strongly vertical monuments to imperialism, or what Joyce calls the "improperial" (*FW* 484.20). This word implies the estrangement from the self as (an admittedly constructed) *propria persona* brought about by colonizing desire, whether on an individual or a national scale; it expresses the alienated condition of the imperial project, with its panoply of masks and rhetorical gestures. The otherness of phallic desire has its bodily signifier in the male erection, which, from a certain perspective, can call into question the identity of the subject in his unique and absolute difference from the non-self. Beckett writes in *First Love* that man is "at the mercy of an erection. . . . one is no longer oneself on such occasions, and it is painful to be no longer oneself, even more painful if possible than when one is (18; quoted in Lloyd 49–50).

*   *   *

The *Wake*'s most extended parody of colonial discourse is the monologue that ends the third chapter of book 3, published separately in 1930 as "Haveth Childers Everywhere" (*FW* 532.6–554.10). Roland McHugh describes this section as "an eloquent self-vindication by the founder, architect, viceroy and Lord Mayor of Dublin telescoped into one person" (1976, 20). His speech covers a number of key events in the colonization of Ireland: the invasion by the Danes in the eighth century; the conquest by the English under Henry II in 1172; the submission of the Irish chieftains to

Henry VIII in 1542; and the suppression of the uprising of 1798. Although Dublin is preeminent, the speech expands to scenes of conquest and colonial rule all over the world, including places like "Corkcutta," part of the association of Ireland with India that forms a running motif throughout the *Wake*. This imperialist version of HCE contrasts with the somewhat put-upon hero of book 1 by revealing him as the "grandada of all rogues" (Joyce in Ellmann 617n) and, in the words of McHugh, "a sadistic instrument of oppression" (1976, 22) whose grandiose claims tend to cancel one another out.

The monologue thus serves as a paradigmatic instance of a colonizing discourse. Where the speaker boasts that he will "westerneyes those poor sunuppers and outbreighton their land's eng" (*FW* 537.11), he proposes to bring both Western views and the enlightenment of English to the benighted Orientals. When he proclaims, "I . . . vanced imperial standard by weaponright and platzed mine residenze" (*FW* 539.19), he recalls the raising of the imperial standard over Dublin Castle following the Act of Union in 1801. In ever-expanding self-congratulation, he claims, "I sent my boundary to Botany Bay and I ran up a score and four of mes while the Yanks were huckling the Empire" (*FW* 543.4). The movement is both outward and upward; geographic expansion combines with prolific fatherhood to show the literally phallic nature of colonial conquest.

It is precisely this phallic "showing" that I will examine in the light of HCE's "alleged misdemeanour" (*FW* 35.6), the infamous if obscure transgression that serves throughout the *Wake* as a running parody of Original Sin. Although the crime is never named, the endless discussion of it revolves around scenes of indecent exposure and voyeurism, two gestures that mirror each other in what has been called the scopic economy of male desire, and that, as I shall argue, Joyce's language connects to the discourse of colonization.

The scene of indecent exposure serves as many purposes in *Finnegans Wake* as it has varying sources. For example, the repeated identification of HCE with the biblical figure of Adam serves Joyce's critique of the doctrine of Original Sin, recalling the moment in Genesis when Adam and Eve cover themselves, their bodily shame symbolizing the broken covenant with God (Gen. 3.7). Joyce's hero reverses that moment by uncovering himself in a literally shameless display, as if to declare his freedom from Original Sin and to reclaim his Edenic innocence.

Since Richard von Krafft-Ebing's classic work on deviant sexuality, *Psychopathia Sexualis* (1886), is often cited as background for some of the more lurid scenes of *Ulysses*,[2] it is surprising that no one before now has seen it as an inspiration for HCE's notorious crime in the park. In one of his case studies, Krafft-Ebing tells the story of a thirty-seven-year-old man, who, excited by alcohol, found pleasure by exhibiting himself in a city park:

> After drawing up his shirt, he posted himself in the shrubbery, and when two women came up the path he approached them with ex-posed genitals. In such exhibition he had a pleasurable feeling of warmth, and the blood mounted to his head. (520)

The case has parallels with several aspects of HCE's alleged transgression in Phoenix Park: his "swallowall" shirt, the setting in the "people's park," the concealment in a "rushy hollow," the scandalized "pair of dainty maid-servants," and the act itself, which was, in the words of an admittedly un-reliable apologist for HCE, "admittedly an incautious but, at its wildest, a partial exposure" (*FW* 33.7–34.27). Readers of the *Wake* will also recog-nize the parallels between HCE's character and this biographical descrip-tion of Krafft-Ebing's exhibitionist:

> From childhood he was eccentric and imaginative. He loved romances about knights and others, was entirely absorbed by them, and even went so far as to identify himself in fancy with the heroes. He always thought himself a little better than others, and thought much of el-egant dress and ornaments; and when he strutted about on Sundays he imagined himself a high official. (520)

Krafft-Ebing's case study combines three motifs that resonate with one another throughout Joyce's work: exhibitionism, chivalric fantasy, and in-stitutional ostentation.

In his analysis of the psychodynamics of colonial rule in Algeria, Frantz Fanon remarks of the colonial settler: "He is an exhibitionist. His preoccu-pation with security makes him remind the native out loud that there he alone is master" (53). If we translate this situation to the individual uncon-scious, what Fanon calls the preoccupation with security corresponds to the castration complex in Freud. According to Freud, the fear of castration underlies the exhibitionist's compulsion: "It is a means of constantly in-sisting upon the integrity of the subject's own (male) genitals and it reiter-ates his infantile satisfaction at the absence of a penis in those of women" (1975, 23). The compulsion to expose oneself therefore would not exist if the exhibitionist did not secretly identify with the woman, whom he sees as the victim of castration he fears himself to be. Likewise the colonizer would not constantly "remind the native out loud" of his superior position if he did not, at some level, recognize his own essential powerlessness. This need continually to reassert his superiority relates to what elsewhere I have called the rhetoric of affirmation, deployed on behalf of a colonizing people who idealize themselves variously in the name of civilization, progress, humanity, science, and so on, so that the repeated affirmation of these ideals becomes in itself a means of maintaining power and mastery (Spurr 109–29).

Just as, for Freud, exhibitionism has its counterpart in voyeurism, so the history of colonial expositions and displays have their counterpart in the economy of the colonizing gaze, which maintains a system of surveillance over the landscapes, domestic interiors, and bodies of the colonized. Grand-scale projects like the Colonial and Indian Exhibition, held in London in 1886, or the Exposition Coloniale Internationale, held in Paris in 1931, combined displays of imperial wealth and achievement with imitation native villages and Oriental streets, complete with whirling dervishes and belly dancers (Greenhalgh 102; Mitchell 217). The result was, in the words of one historian, "the ordering up of the world itself as an endless exhibition" (Mitchell 218). In *Finnegans Wake*, HCE's imperial conquest is followed by his construction of a "city of magnificent distances" (*FW* 539.25) complete with pageants, exhibitions, and pantomimes, and food imported from exotic lands. This imperial construction includes the vision of penetration, or the penetration of vision, into the interior space of the Oriental harem, a fantasy explored by Western artists from Charles de Montesquieu (*Les Lettres persanes*) to Federico Fellini (*Amarcord*). Thus HCE's version: "in my bethel of Solyman's I accouched their rotundaties and I turnkeyed most insultantly over raped lutetias in the lock" (*FW* 542.27–29). The invasion and unveiling of this eroticized Oriental space is merely the obverse of the exhibitionist display.

Indecent exposure, however, is a crime not because it offends women but because it offends men: it quite literally exposes the underpinnings of masculine authority and desire, revealing them as manifestations of an inherent anxiety, a male hysteria. The same is true of excessive displays of colonial power. Warren Hastings, the first governor general of British India, was brought to trial not for his offenses to India but for his offense to Great Britain in having laid bare the force that underlies colonial rule everywhere. Joyce is able to conflate the crime of indecent exposure with that of imperial hubris because they amount to the same thing. Both are aspects of a discourse that, as Irigaray observes, necessarily represents phallic desire (77).

In "Haveth Childers Everywhere," the speaker recklessly shifts registers, veering from confident expressions of imperial authority to ineffectual denials of petty perversions. When he states, "I am known throughout the world wherever my good Allenglisches Angleslachsen is spoken" (*FW* 532.9–11), the notion of a "good English" may be undermined by the allusion to its diverse linguistic origins, but the worldly tone prepares for the broadcast of this same voice on the airwaves of the BBC: "Calm has entered. Big big calm, announcer" (*FW* 534.7). As a single voice resounding calmly over the globe, the monologic authority of the British Broadcasting Corporation corresponds in its power of dissemination to HCE's capacity to populate the earth with the seed of his loins.

The voice of the BBC resounds as an aural counterpart to the visual display of the world embodied in the grand exhibitions. Both are aspects of the distinctly modern phenomenon defined by Heidegger in which the world is "conceived and grasped as a picture" by human beings who derive their very subjectivity from this representational power. For Heidegger, this is a distinctly modern phenomenon, in which "man" constitutes himself as "that particular being who gives the measure and draws up the guidelines for everything that is" (134), recalling HCE's heroic construction, in the closing pages of "Haveth Childers Everywhere," of palaces, spires, monuments, boulevards, ports, gardens, vineyards, villas, breweries, universities, and codes of law.

Radio broadcasts belong to that dimension of the production of the worldview that Heidegger calls the gigantic:

> The gigantic presses forward in a form that actually seems to make it disappear—in the annihilation of great distances by the airplane, in the setting before us of foreign and remote worlds in their everydayness, which is produced at random through radio by a flick of the hand. (135)

Gigantism, however, is more than just a quantitative phenomenon, just as the radio broadcast and the phonograph recording are more than simply extensions of voice through space and time; rather, they alter profoundly the nature of space and time. Gigantism thus has an incalculable quality, an "invisible shadow" by means of which "the modern world extends itself out into a space withdrawn from representation" (136). It is a modern paradox that the triumph of representation in the form of gigantism produces, in spite of itself, a space of the unrepresentable and incalculable, of otherness. The sheer power and extension of the BBC, like that of the British Empire itself, were such that the system's effects could be neither predicted nor controlled.

Joyce captures this self-sabotaging effect of gigantism in the imperial locutions that are invariably compromised by dubious protestations of innocence in the confessional mode: "I never was nor can afford to be guilty of crim crig con of malfeasance trespass against parson with the person of a youthful gigirl frifrif friend" (FW 532.18–20). The imperial adventure of the Crimean War, *Krim Krieg* in German, here is implicated, literally folded into the tawdry scene of sexual misconduct. Likewise, the Olympian composure of the BBC announcer is disturbed by stammering efforts to clear his reputation that tend only toward self-incrimination: "I contango can take off my dudud dirtynine articles of quoting here in Pynix Park before those in heaven to provost myself, by gramercy of justness, I mean veryman and moremon, stiff and staunch forever" (FW 534.11–14).

In the phenomenon described by Derrida as "double writing" there is a displacement that takes place "whenever any writing both marks and goes back over its mark with an undecidable stroke" (1981, 143). Like a palimpsest, it "writes over" itself in a gesture that both conceals and reveals another sign. HCE's dubious testimony is double writing with a vengeance. In hiding behind the thirty-nine articles of the Church of England, another pillar of empire, his intended act of concealment reenacts the remembered act of revealment: the taking off of his dirty articles of clothing in Phoenix Park. The act is again both obscured and revealed by reference to "the best begrudged man in Belgradia who does not belease to our paviour" (FW 534.21–23) a condensed version of a limerick for which McHugh's *Annotations* provide the full text:

> There was a young man from Belgravia
> Who believed not in God nor in Saviour.
> He walked down the Strand
> With his balls in his hand
> And was had up for indecent behaviour.
> (1991, 534)

Indignant at being had up for a similar offense, HCE offers to swear an oath by the Long Stone, the pillar in Dublin marking the place where the Danes landed in the eighth century. Inevitably, however, his language betrays him by reliving the scandalous scene in the park: "I will . . . testify to my unclothed virtue by the longstone erectheion of our allfirst manhere" (*FW* 538.34–539.4). By linking the origins of colonial domination in Ireland to HCE's own "shrubbery trick," Joyce exposes to view both the erotic formations of empire and the imperialist dimensions of masculine desire.

The uncontrolled effects of HCE's language make it a spectacular example of the inherent ambivalence of colonial discourse, which arises out of the collision between what Freud identifies as two distinct psychic motives in language: one takes reality into account, while the other seeks to replace it with an object of desire. When language itself effaces this distinction between reality and wish-fulfillment, the result is what Homi Bhabha, borrowing from both Freud and Derrida, calls the *Entstellung,* or disfigurement, of colonial discourse: "domination is achieved through a process of disavowal that denies the *différance* of colonialist power—the chaos of its intervention as *Entstellung,* its dislocatory presence" (1985, 153). Heisenberg's uncertainty principle—in which the investigation of a natural phenomenon alters the phenomenon itself—applies to colonialism as well as to scientific observation; the logic of authority breaks down when its presence alters in unpredictable ways the intended object of authority. The disfigured and continually self-displacing formations of HCE's discourse thus mark a split within the voice of authority itself: on one hand, it represents itself as occupying the space of colonization with a total and unitary presence; on the other, it betrays a desire for that *other* presence, within or without, that escapes its dominion.

To say that the *Wake* marks a split within a generalized voice of authority raises the question of the critical and parodic functions of Joyce's work. If colonial discourse already sabotages itself, what exactly is the nature of the *Wake*'s subversion? The answer may be found in the ambivalent relation between a parody and its object, according to which the former is neither independent of nor identical to the latter. The conditions for parody are always inherent as possibility in the original text; the parodic form is what makes them manifest. By the same token, the *Wake*'s grandiloquent mimicry of colonial discourse dramatizes for comic effect the disfigurement and chaos already present within the discourse. This point can only be made, however, with the reservation that such oppositions of parody and object, latency and manifestation can serve only as provisional models for a text the form of which cannot really be captured by recourse to binary models. *Finnegans Wake* is, for example, a parody for which there is no original text, the notion of textual origin, with its claims to historicity and uniqueness, having been overwhelmed by the theoretically simultaneous presence and intercontamination of all texts in Joyce's work.

*   *   *

We have seen how in HCE Joyce represents colonial authority in terms of a transgressive male sexuality. In the figure of HCE's wife, ALP (for Anna Livia Plurabelle), however, he shows that the object of this transgression is always incompletely colonized in its feminine plurality and fluidity, remaining a voice whose "style," in the words of Luce Irigaray, "resists and explodes every firmly established form, figure, idea or concept" (79). The splitting and fragmentation of the colonial sign under the pressure of an uncolonized other has to do with what Bhabha calls the "*uncanny* of cultural difference" (1990, 313). Cultural difference does not simply represent the tension between opposing traditions of cultural value. Rather, difference is already there within the sign of cultural value as the ungathered residue, the intractable material that representation effaces, the loss of meaning registered in the articulation of the sign itself. This is not a simple question of repression but of an otherness, an internal difference within the structures of linguistic representation, an irreducible strangeness with which the speaker is nonetheless intimate. In the classic colonial situation, this strange and intractable material is the cultural other that, though projected *out there*, is nonetheless latent in the ambivalent structures of the colonizing discourse. In gender relations, this same material has been made invisible by the formations of masculine logic. In both cases this lost, strange, and disturbingly multiple otherness constitutes the object of desire.

In the pages that lead up to "Haveth Childers Everywhere," the "drama parapolylogic" of III.3 joins the voice of the feminine to the site of colonization and suggests that the agonistic relation between colonizer and colonized is not one of antithetical opposition but of profound ambivalence. *Ambivalence*, again, is a less than satisfactory word for the unpredictable ways in which authority alters the conditions of its own presence. To put things in narrative order, this is the chapter in which the four judges (also known as Matthew, Mark, Luke, and John, or as Mamalujo, collectively) perform an inquisition on the somnolent personage named Yawn (a version of HCE's son Shaun) in their quest for HCE and the true nature of his crime in the park. Their efforts seem about to be rewarded [*He drapped his draraks on Mansianhase parak* (*FW* 491.18)] when the proceedings are interrupted by the voice of ALP, who begs "to traverse same above statement" by offering what looks like an alibi for her husband: at the time of the alleged misdemeanor he was "confined to guardroom," that is, drunk in bed (McHugh, 1991) "due to Zenaphiah Holwell" (*FW* 492.18), that is, John Zephaniah Holwell, commanding officer of the British garrison at Calcutta besieged by Bengali forces in 1756.

ALP's speech is filled with references to the British raj, Hindu culture, and two famous episodes of resistance to British colonial rule. In 1756, the nawab of Bengal, Siraj-ud-daula, captured the British garrison under Holwell's command at Calcutta. According to a story that became saturated with imperial feeling, 146 Europeans were confined overnight in the garrison's small, stifling guardroom. Lord Macaulay describes the appalling scene in an essay on which Joyce was required to write for his B.A. examination in 1899 (Davison):

> Then the prisoners went mad with despair. They trampled each other down, fought for the places at the windows, fought for the pittance of water with which the cruel mercy of the murderers mocked their agonies, raved, prayed, blasphemed, implored the guards to fire among them. (Macaulay 223–24)

The next morning only twenty-three persons remained alive in the chamber, which became infamous as the Black Hole of Calcutta.

The other episode, much larger in scope, is the Sepoy Rebellion of 1857, when native soldiers of the East India Company mutinied, captured the cities of Delhi and Lucknow, and massacred the British colony at Cawnpore. The British reprisals that followed equaled or exceeded the rebellion itself in their atrocity, but in Britain and British India these events became the central elements of an imperialist hagiography: the European victims were considered martyrs to the cause of empire. Along with the Battle of Plassey—which inaugurated British rule in 1757—the Black Hole and the Mutiny were the things that "every schoolboy knew" about India (V. Smith 429). The Black Hole itself became a metonymic figure for Calcutta and ultimately for the unfathomable depths of India itself, like Kipling's "City of Dreadful Night" and the Marabar Caves of Forster's *A Passage to India*.

As ALP evokes memories of these events, her speech is joined to the discourse of colonization, while at the same time subverting it through a series of displacements and deformations that testify to the intervention, within the discourse, of the colonized other. The result is an elaborate example of what Bhabha calls the colonial hybrid, where authority is both avowed and estranged from itself. The context of ALP's speech as a defense of her husband adds another dimension to this ambiguity, offering parallels between colonial and conjugal relations: both combine scenes of violence and revenge with feelings of intimacy and desire.

In Joyce's text, the Black Hole of Calcutta becomes the "back haul of Coalcutter," the dark matter mined from the depths of consciousness, where the wife's vision of her husband is the "hindustanding" of the colonial subject, mixing affectionate with murderous impulses. Aided by the nawab of Bengal disguised as the "chemist and family drugger, Surager Dowling, V.S." [Veterinary Surgeon], she ministers to her ailing husband with a "pint of his Filthered pilsens bottle," an ambivalent prescription having the undecidable effects of the *pharmakon*, both medicinal tonic and "slow poisoning" (*FW* 492.16–18).

ALP's role as the colonized Hindu provokes her to write "in mepetition" (that is, petition as self-repetition) to "Kavanagh Djanaral," a figure who adds to a recurring theme of disguise. Kavanagh Djanaral is the governor general and thus HCE, as well as Thomas Henry Kavanagh, a spy whose exploits in native disguise helped the British recapture Lucknow during the Mutiny. His disguise is equalled in audacity, if not in valor, by another historical personage, a certain Patrick Joyce, who passed as a Turk named Achmet Borumborad while maintaining a Dublin bathhouse (Tindall 279). Joyce-Borumborad surfaces here as an Indian sahib and "aural surgeon," presumably for the pierced ear of HCE, who momentarily appears under the alias of a certain Erill Pearcey.

Kavanagh and Borumborad are instances of a hybrid figure recurring throughout the *Wake* that identifies the Irish with the Indian as objects of colonial domination. The book's first chapter takes us on a tour of the "Willingdone Museyroom" memorializing the Dublin-born Duke of Wellington's early military campaigns in India. As Vincent Cheng points out, the "hinndoo" encountered in the tour is an amalgam of two Irishmen, Hinnessy and Dooley, while his proper name, Shimar Shin, orientalizes Shem and Shaun, the two sons of HCE and ALP. The hinndoo's resentment of the colonizer may be compared to that of the Irish soldier Buckley. The latter watches a Russian general defecate on the Crimean battlefield and then wipe himself with a piece of its turf. In Buckley's confused eye, however, the general stands for the perennial invader, now insulting Ireland's green sod in an unforgivable manner. Thus the "insoult" that the hinndoo suffers from Willingdone's "big wide harse" (*FW* 10.11–14) is equivalent, in both political and scatological content, to the "instullt to Igorladns," which later provokes Buckley to shoot the Russian general (*FW* 353.18).

As for ALP, her grievance against her "rupee repure riputed husbandship" (*FW* 492.36) is tempered with loving admiration, so that what Campbell and Robinson describe as the complaint of a "raped India" (22) sounds more like the celebration of carnal pleasure between a robust maharini and her dutiful maharajah:

> he never battered one eagle's eye before paying me his duty . . . but he hidded up my hemifaces in all my mayarannies and he locked plum into my mirrymouth . . . with the light's hope on his ruddycheeks and rawjaws and, my charmer, whom I dipped my hand in, he simply showed me his propendiculous loadpoker. (*FW* 493.3–10)

This last piece of virile equipment recalls ALP's earlier reference to her man as "my dodear devere revered mainhirr," a menhir being, according to the *Oxford English Dictionary,* "a tall upright monumental stone, of varying antiquity, found in parts of Europe, and in Africa and Asia." The obelisk has indeed risen, but the odalisque has not exactly fallen; rather she plays an enthusiastic part in its erection. The imperial HCE, meanwhile, has gone magnificently native. The "wisest of the Vikramadityationists" or Hindu patrons of the arts, he now speaks in "gulughurutty," apparently a Gogarty version of the Gujurati language of India.[3]

The point is not to minimize the violence of colonial rule, but to show how Joyce's writing brings out the uncanny and unmanageable effects of colonial authority, which compromise its intended uniformity and clarity, thus estranging authority from itself. In the case of the Hinduized ALP, Joyce creates this sense of estrangement through the strategies of repetition, mimicry, and hyperbole available to the voice of the colonized. Here the denied discourse of feminine desire disrupts the uniform structure of authority by returning the gaze and fetishizing the sign of masculine desire. The result is a radical dislocation of the colonizing discourse and its exposure as the space of a double inscription. As Derrida says of discourse in a related context, it "plays a double scene upon a double stage" (1991, 190), the same syntax both establishing authority and preparing the ground for authority's subversion.

Recent work in the theory of colonial discourse has arrived at a moment of confrontation between two opposing critical approaches. On one side are

those who see the ideology of discourse as expressing political and economic forces that operate independently of language. On the other side are
those who focus on discourse itself as social practice and seek to uncover
the concealed workings of ideology by "stirring up and dispersing the
sedimented meanings dormant in texts" (Parry 32). Where the first group
considers language as merely one of the effects of power, the other sees
language and power as inseparable.

As Benita Parry points out, neither approach has produced a new discourse that would supersede the modes of knowledge informing past and
present forms of Western imperialism. Where discourse is only the effect
of material and social conditions, there is no way for new kinds of language
to create conditions that do not yet exist. Where discourse is understood to
be as universal as power itself, the space from which to create opposition
lies inside rather than outside its structures. Thus critics devoted to this
latter project, like Bhabha and Gayatri Spivak, seem destined "to place incendiary devices within the dominant structures of representation and not
to confront these with another knowledge" (43).

If we are to consider Joyce as a prototheorist of colonial discourse, he
would seem to belong to the incendiary camp that equates language with
power itself, and whose own discourse thus conducts a kind a guerrilla
warfare with traditional and dominant modes of writing. In an essay on
Joyce's anarchist sympathies, Dominic Manganiello points out that "Joyce
recognizes no essential distinction between a view of history and a view of
language" (114). Where the political, the sexual, and the national are constituted by and through language, the visionary artist perhaps alone has
the power to shatter and recreate these categories. In a related observation,
the Syrian critic Sadik Al-Azm has noted that what connects Joyce to more
recent postcolonial writers such as Salman Rushdie is his "heightened sen-
sitivity to the fact that he was writing about Ireland in a language other
than his own, thus enriching the oppressors' literary treasury" (Al-Azm
1991). The resistance to this role leads both writers to produce multi-
lingual works that systematically sabotage traditional literary English
through their "heteroglossia (to use Bakhtin's term) and copious inter-
lingual play on words, *double-entendre,* puns and slang usages" (Al-Azm
1991). Joyce's alliance with the saboteurs of colonizing discourse would
conform to the disruptive tactics of Shem the Penman, of whom it is written, "he would wipe alley english spooker, multaphoniaksically spuking,
off the face of the erse" (*FW* 178.6). That is, he would wipe any English
speaker off the face of the earth; he would whip the imperial general's ass;

he would exorcise the haunting ghost ("spooker") of English through a vomited speech ("spuking") of dislocations and adulterations. This alliance would also confirm that the catastrophe referred to in book 2 as the "ab-nihilisation of the etym" (*FW* 353.22) provides a metaphor for the *Wake* itself, and for its author, who "having murdered all the English he knew, picked out his pockets and left the tribunal scotfree" (*FW* 93.2). I would ultimately argue, however, that Joyce annihilates the English language precisely in order to re-create, so that the inspired non-sense of the colonial subject is remade into a visionary order where English is read and spoken from a wholly new perspective: "Behove this sound of Irish sense. Really? Here English might be seen. Royally? . . . Hush! Caution! Echoland!" (*FW* 22.36–23.5). This three-word reading of the name of HCE represents a subtle but meaningful advance over the threefold strategy of "silence, exile, and cunning" (*P* 247) that Stephen Dedalus adopts in *A Portrait of the Artist as a Young Man.* Silence and cunning are still present in "hush" and "caution," but exile has been replaced by the epiphanic "echoland," as if the wandering figure of Joyce's earlier work had found a home in the sonorous reverberations of the world as it is called forth in language.

Seen in this light, the "postcoloniality" of *Finnegans Wake* lies in its affirmative as well as its disruptive force; and here a final comparison with Beckett is in order. The postcolonial quality of Beckett's work resides in what Lloyd calls his "perpetuation of difference against ideological identifications" (Lloyd 55), an aesthetic of nonidentity (with patriarchy, nation, empire) pursued through artistic strategies of negation and ascesis. *Finnegans Wake* achieves the same effect through an opposite but sympathetic strategy of combination and affirmation—the affirmation of a perpetual revealment in language that is equally resistant to ideological identifications. Such a strategy imitates the encyclopedic scope of imperialist discourse precisely in order to dislocate its classificatory structures. The project of the *Wake* is finally to evoke a linguistic universe no longer bound by colonial relations of power; these unhappy relations are the nightmare of history from which Joyce's work calls us to awake.

Notes

Introduction: Altereffects

A note on Derrida's *Ulysse gramophone: Deux mots pour Joyce* (Galilée, 1987): This book contains two essays in French. The first, "Deux mots pour Joyce," was first published in an English translation (of an unpublished French transcript) by Geoff Bennington in Derek Attridge and Daniel Ferrer, eds., *Post-Structuralist Joyce*, 145–59. What is published in the Galilée 1987 edition is a later, French version of the same essay.

The second essay, "Ulysse gramophone: Ouï-dire de Joyce," is printed here in the French, for which there is no published translation. In quoting from the first essay, I cite Bennington's 1984 translation. In quoting from the second, I cite it as it appears (in French) in the 1987 Galilée edition, 57–143. Translations of this essay are my own.

Chapter 1. Colonial Spaces in Joyce's Dublin

1. See Edward Morel's *Red Rubber*, a journalistic exposé of conditions in the rubber plantations of the Congo in 1906.

2. See, for example, Vincent Cheng (1993, 31) and the commentary on his reading of "The Dead" by Patrick Ledden.

3. The architecture of Trinity College is similarly treated in *Ulysses*, where Leopold Bloom views "Trinity's surly front" (*U* 8.476) from College Green. The context is again that of colonial institutions, as Bloom has just been thinking of the Bank of Ireland. For this and other helpful observations, I am grateful to Fritz Senn of the Zürich James Joyce Foundation.

4. Citations to Dante's *Divine Comedy* refer to the Italian text with facing English translation, in three volumes, by John D. Sinclair (New York: Oxford University Press, 1961). Canto and line numbers are given for the Italian; page numbers are given for the translation.

Chapter 2. The Comedy of Intolerance in Proust and Joyce

1. Citations to Proust's *A la recherche du temps perdu* refer to the 1988 edition edited by Jean-Yves Tadié (Paris: Gallimard, Editions de la Pléiade). Citations to the English translation of this work refer to the 1981 translation by C. K. Scott Moncrieff and Terence Kilmartin (New York: Random House).

2. Japheth, the third son of Noah, is sometimes considered to be the ancestor of the Indo-Europeans, therefore of the non-Jews.

3. "Ireland, Island of Saints and Sages" is the title of a public lecture Joyce gave in Trieste in 1907. It is published in his *Critical Writings*.

Chapter 3. Anthropologies of Modernism: Joyce, Eliot, Lévy-Bruhl

1. Eliot was a constant and enthusiastic supporter of Joyce's work, beginning with the publication in the *Egoist* (June–July 1918) of sections from *Ulysses,* a work that had its impact on the writing of *The Waste Land.* As editor of the *Criterion* and at Faber and Faber, Eliot published parts of *Work in Progress,* as well as the completed *Finnegans Wake* in 1939. For his part, Joyce remained wary of Eliot but paid him a kind of homage through his parodies of *The Waste Land,* both in *Finnegans Wake* and in a letter to Harriet Shaw Weaver (Ellmann 572). Sultan's *Eliot, Joyce and Company* is a recent and authoritative study of relations between the two writers; it provides a bibliography (138 n) of studies comparing *The Waste Land* and *Finnegans Wake.* See Tindall for allusions to Eliot's poem in the *Wake.*

2. In writing of anthropology, I refer to the discipline known in the 1920s as cultural anthropology in America, social anthropology in Britain, and ethnology in France. Eliot's use of the latter term, despite his debt to Frazer, conforms to his orientation toward the French school and the work of Lévy-Bruhl in particular, part of whose work on primitive mentality he would publish in the *Criterion* (February 1924).

3. In her reading of Paul de Kock's *Ruby, Pride of the Ring,* Molly puzzles over the word, which she pronounces "met him pike hoses." Bloom provides a definition: "from the Greek. That means the transmigration of souls" (*U* 4.341–42).

4. Jules Monnerot's *La poésie moderne et le sacré* has an extended discussion of surrealism in the context of Lévy-Bruhl's theories (97–120). This essay is cited by Breton in a 1946 interview where he acknowledges the affinity of the surrealist vision with the primitive (1969, 244–45). For other discussions of the surrealists' appropriation of the primitive, see Charles Wentinck's chapter titled "Surrealism and the Art of the South Sea Islands" (27–30); Robert Goldwater (216–24); Anna Balakian (152–54); and notably, Evan Maurer's essay in the catalogue for the 1984 Museum of Modern Art exhibit titled *"Primitivism" in Twentieth-Century Art: Affinity of the Tribal and the Modern.*

5. In contrast to his regard for Lévy-Bruhl's intellectual contribution, Eliot valued *The Golden Bough* precisely for its presentation of factual material unencumbered by theoretical speculation (1924a, 29). Several writers have discussed the form

of Frazer's work, with its comparative juxtapositions, as a model for Eliot's poetry, especially *The Waste Land*. See John Vickery (235–36); Piers Gray (131–32); and Marc Manganaro (1992, 68f.). Manganaro notes Frazer's "textual dependence that encouraged the profusion of myriad voices, sources, cultures, epochs," a model superseded by Malinowski's method of participant observation of a single culture (69).

6. This handwritten paper comprises section (*b*) of the volume titled "Philosophical Essays" in the John Hayward bequest of T. S. Eliot materials in the Library of King's College, Cambridge. Gray, who rediscovered the manuscript, quotes it at length.

7. Crawford provides an extended discussion of the savage in Eliot's work, focusing on "his linking of the most primitive with the most sophisticatedly urban" (2).

8. Manganaro (1986, 108) finds a source for the "dead land" of this poem in *Les fonctions mentales*, where Lévy-Bruhl discusses the "pays des morts" of West African folklore (84).

9. Ricks, in his discussion of Eliot's anti-Semitism, cites two theories related to the one I propose here. Graham Martin remarks that "when [Eliot] was still struggling to attach himself to an acceptable version of English society (in the deepest sense), the uncultured Jew functioned as a whipping boy for his own suppressed self" (Ricks 28n). More ingeniously, William Empson finds an Oedipal source of Eliot's anti-Semitism in feelings of resentment toward his Unitarian father: "Now if you are hating a purse-proud businessman who denies that Jesus is God, into what stereotype does he best fit?" (Ricks 47). In a letter to J. V. Healy (see note 10 below), Eliot compared the Jewish religion, "shorn of its traditional practices," to "a mild and colourless form of Unitarianism" (Ricks 44).

Anti-Semitism can sometimes be literally decoded in Eliot's poems. In "Gerontion," for example, the Jew who squats on the windowsill has been "[s]pawned in some estaminet of Antwerp" (1952, 21). I am indebted to Ned Lukacher, and to the students in his seminar "Anti-Semitism and Literature," for the observation that "estaminet" is an anagram for "anti-Semite."

10. Eliot's own explanation of the notorious phrase, quoted in Ricks (44), is not very helpful: "By free-thinking Jews I mean Jews who have given up the practice and belief of their own religion, without having become Christians or attached themselves to any other dogmatic religion. It should be obvious that I think a large number of free-thinkers of any race to be undesirable, and the free-thinking Jews are only a special case" (May 10, 1940, letter to J. V. Healy, at the Harry Ransom Humanities Research Center, University of Texas at Austin).

11. Don Gifford suggests as a possible source for this wedding rite a work he cites as William Ellis's *Three Trips to Madagascar* (London, 1838), which is listed in the "Ithaca" chapter of *Ulysses* as an item in Bloom's private library, but with "title obliterated" (*U* 17.1374). This work, in fact titled *Three Visits to Madagascar*, contains no reference to any rite resembling the one described in "Oxen of the Sun."

12. Joyce's Jones bears resemblance both to Sir William Jones, the great eighteenth-century Orientalist, and to Ernest Jones, the psychoanalyst and interpreter

of Freud. Though best known in literary studies for his work on *Hamlet,* Ernest Jones also wrote essays on anthropology, on the "Jewish question," and on the character traits of the Irish and Welsh. In "The Inferiority Complex of the Welsh," Jones compares his compatriots to the Jews. See his *Essays in Applied Psycho-Analysis.*

Chapter 4. Joyce, *Hamlet,* Mallarmé

1. Citations to William Shakespeare's *Hamlet* refer to act, scene, and line.

Chapter 7. Writing in the *Wake* of Empire

1. An early study in this vein was that of Colin MacCabe. For a more recent example, see the collection of essays edited by Vincent Cheng and Timothy Martin.

2. Krafft-Ebing is a familiar source for the scenes of masochism, coprophilia, and fetishism in the "Circe" episode of *Ulysses,* while the "pleasurable feeling of warmth" described here is similar to the effect of reading pornography on Bloom's body in "Wandering Rocks": "Warmth showered gently over him, cowing his flesh" (*U* 10.619).

3. Oliver St. John Gogarty, sometime companion of Joyce in Dublin, became a nemesis of the young writer, who later portrayed him as Buck Mulligan in *Ulysses.*

References

Ackroyd, Peter. 1984. *T. S. Eliot: A life.* New York: Simon and Schuster.

Adorno, Theodor W. 1991. *Notes to literature.* Translated by S. H. Nicholsen. New York: Columbia University Press.

Al-Azm, Sadik. 1991. The importance of being earnest about Salman Rushdie. *Die Welt des Islams* 31 (1991). Quoted in Christopher Hitchens, Diary, *London Review of Books* 24 (February 1994): 29.

Althusser, Louis. 1965. *Lire le capital.* Paris: F. Maspero.

Arnold, Matthew. 1970. On the modern element in literature. In *Selected prose,* edited by P. J. Keating. London: Penguin.

Auster, Paul. 1985. *City of glass.* In *The New York trilogy.* New York: Penguin.

Balakian, Anna. 1971. *André Breton: Magus of surrealism.* New York: Oxford University Press.

Barthes, Roland. 1974. *S/Z: An essay.* Translated by Richard Miller. New York: Hill and Wang.

Bataille, Georges. 1988. Marcel Proust. In *Oeuvres complètes,* vol. 11, 391–94. Paris: Gallimard.

Baudelaire, Charles. 1962. *Curiosités esthétiques, l'art romantique, et autres oeuvres critiques.* Paris: Garnier.

———. 1975. *Oeuvres complètes.* Paris: Pléiade.

———. 1981. The painter of modern life. In *Selected writings on art and artists,* translated by P. E. Charvet. Cambridge: Cambridge University Press.

Baum, L. Frank. 1900. *The wonderful wizard of Oz.* Chicago: D. M. Hill.

Beckett, Samuel. 1931. *Proust.* New York: Grove.

———. 1970. *First love and other stories.* New York: Grove.

Beckett, Samuel, Marcel Brion, Frank Budgen, Stuart Gilbert, Eugene Jolas, Victor Llona, Robert McAlmon, Thomas McGreevy, Elliott Paul, John Rodker, Robert Sage, and William Carlos Williams. 1962. *Our exagmination round his factification for incamination of "Work in Progress."* Paris: Shakespeare and Co. 1929. Reprint, New York: New Directions.

Bem, Jeanne. 1980. Le juif et l'homosexuel dans *A la recherche du temps perdu. Littérature* 37: 100–112.

Benjamin, Walter. 1969. *Illuminations.* Translated by Harry Zohn. New York: Schocken.

―――. 1986. *Reflections: Essays, aphorisms, autobiographical writings.* Translated by Edmund Jephcott and edited by Peter Demetz. New York: Schocken.

Bhabha, Homi. 1985. Signs taken for wonders: Questions of ambivalence and authority under a tree outside Delhi, May 1817. *Critical Inquiry* 12: 144–65.

―――. 1990. DissemiNation: Time, narrative, and the margins of the modern nation. In *Nation and narration,* edited by Homi Bhabha. London: Routledge.

Blanchot, Maurice. 1949. *La part du feu.* Paris: Gallimard.

―――. 1993. *The infinite conversation.* Translated by Susan Hanson. Minneapolis: University of Minnesota Press.

―――. 1995. The pursuit of the zero point. Translated by Ian Machlachlan. In *The Blanchot reader,* edited by Michael Holland, 143–50. Oxford: Blackwell.

Borges, Jorge Luis. 1988. *Labyrinths.* Translated by Donald A. Yates. New York: Norton.

Breton, André. 1969. *Entretiens 1913–1952.* Paris: Gallimard.

―――. 1973. *Manifestes du surréalisme.* Paris: Gallimard.

Brun, Bernard. 1988. Brouillons et brouillages: Proust et l'antisémitisme. *Littérature* 70: 110–28.

Burton, Robert. 1997. *The anatomy of melancholy.* Edited by Thomas C. Faulkner, Nicolas K. Kiessling, and Rhonda L. Blair. Oxford: Clarendon Press.

Cailliet, Emile, and Jean-Albert Bédé. 1932. Le symbolisme et l'âme primitive. *Revue de littérature comparée* 12: 356–86.

Campbell, Joseph, and Henry Morton Robinson. 1977. *A skeleton key to "Finnegans Wake."* New York: Penguin.

Castle, Terry. 1995. *The female thermometer: Eighteenth-century culture and the invention of the uncanny.* New York: Oxford University Press.

Cazeneuve, Jean. 1972. *Lucien Lévy-Bruhl.* Translated by Peter Rivière. New York: Harper.

Cheng, Vincent. 1992. The general and the sepoy: Imperialism and power in the museyroom. In *Critical Essays on James Joyce's "Finnegans Wake,"* edited by Patrick A. McCarthy, 258–68. New York: G. K. Hall.

―――. 1993. Empire and patriarchy in "The Dead." *Joyce Studies Annual:* 16–42.

Cheng, Vincent, and Timothy Martin, eds. 1992. *Joyce in context.* Cambridge: Cambridge University Press.

Clifford, James. 1988. *The predicament of culture: Twentieth-century ethnography, literature, and art.* Cambridge: Harvard University Press.

Compagnon, Antoine. 1983. *La Troisième République des Lettres: de Flaubert à Proust.* Paris: Seuil.

Connolly, Thomas. 1957. *The personal library of James Joyce.* Buffalo: University of Buffalo Bookstore.

Conrad, Joseph. 1950. *Heart of darkness.* New York: Signet.

Craig, Maurice. 1952. *Dublin: 1660–1860.* London: Cresset Press.

Crawford, Robert. 1987. *The savage and the city in the work of T. S. Eliot*. Oxford: Oxford University Press.

Dante Alighieri. 1961. *The Divine Comedy*. Translated by John D. Sinclair. 3 vols. New York: Oxford University Press.

Davison, Neil R. 1993. Joyce's matriculation examination. *James Joyce Quarterly* 30: 393–407.

Deane, Seamus. 1992. Notes to *A portrait of the artist as a young man*, 277–329. New York: Penguin.

de Certeau, Michel. 1984. *The practice of everyday life*. Translated by Steven Rendall. Berkeley: University of California Press.

de Man, Paul. 1983. *Blindness and insight: Essays in the rhetoric of contemporary criticism*. Minneapolis: University of Minnesota Press.

———. 1989. *Critical writings, 1953–1978*. Minneapolis: University of Minnesota Press.

Derrida, Jacques. 1976. *Of grammatology*. Translated by Gayatri Chakravorty Spivak. Baltimore: Johns Hopkins University Press.

———. 1978. *Writing and difference*. Translated by Alan Bass. Chicago: University of Chicago Press.

———. 1981. *Dissemination*. Translated by Barbara Johnson. Chicago: University of Chicago Press.

———. 1984. Two words for Joyce. Translated by Geoff Bennington. In *Post-structuralist Joyce: Essays from the French*, edited by Derek Attridge and Daniel Ferrer, 145–59. Cambridge: Cambridge University Press.

———. 1987. Ulysse gramophone: Ouï-dire de Joyce. In *Ulysse gramophone: Deux mots pour Joyce*, 57–143. Paris: Galilée.

———. 1991. *A Derrida reader: Between the blinds*. Edited by Peggy Kamuf. New York: Columbia University Press.

Dickens, Charles. 1971. *Bleak House*. London: Penguin.

Diesbach, Ghislain de. 1991. *Proust*. Paris: Perrin.

Dirlik, Arif. 1994. The postcolonial aura: Third world criticism in the age of global capitalism. *Critical Inquiry* 20: 328–56.

Eliot, T. S. 1916. Review of *Group theories of religion and the religion of the individual*, by Clement C. J. Webb. *International Journal of Ethics* 27.1 (October): 115–17.

———. 1924a. A prediction in regard to three English authors, writers who, though masters of thought, are likewise masters of art. *Vanity Fair* (February): 29, 98.

———. 1924b. Review of *The growth of civilization and the origin of magic and religion*, by W. J. Perry. *Criterion* 2.8 (July): 489–91.

———. 1933. *The use of poetry and the use of criticism*. London: Faber and Faber.

———. 1934. *After strange gods*. London: Faber and Faber.

———. 1952. *The complete poems and plays, 1909–1950*. New York: Harcourt.

———. 1968. *Christianity and culture*. New York: Harcourt.

———. 1975. *Selected prose*. Edited by Frank Kermode. New York: Harcourt.

————. 1988. *The letters of T. S. Eliot.* Vol. 1, 1898–1922. Edited by Valerie Eliot. New York: Harcourt.

————. 1989. *Knowledge and experience in the philosophy of F. H. Bradley.* New York: Columbia University Press.

Ellmann, Richard. 1982. *James Joyce.* Oxford: Oxford University Press.

Empson, William. 1984. *Using biography.* London: Chatto and Windus.

Ervine, St. John. 1925. *Parnell.* London: Ernest Benn.

Eysteinsson, Astradur. 1990. *The concept of modernism.* Ithaca, N.Y.: Cornell University Press.

Fanon, Frantz. 1968. *The wretched of the earth.* Translated by Constance Farrington. New York: Grove.

Fitch, Noel Riley. 1988. "The first *Ulysses.*" In *The augmented Ninth: Proceedings of the Ninth International James Joyce Symposium*, edited by Bernard Benstock. Syracuse: Syracuse University Press.

Forster, E. M. 1952. *A passage to India.* 1924. New York: Harcourt.

Foucault, Michel. 1970. *The order of things: An archaeology of the human sciences.* New York: Vintage.

————. 1977. *Discipline and punish: The birth of the prison.* Translated by Alan Sheridan. New York: Pantheon.

————. 1980a. The eye of power: A conversation with Jean-Pierre Barou and Michelle Perrot. Translated by Colin Gordon. In *Power/knowledge: Selected interviews and other writings 1972–1977*, edited by Colin Gordon, 146–65. New York: Pantheon.

————. 1980b. *The history of sexuality I: An introduction.* New York: Vintage.

————. 1984. Space, knowledge, and power. Translated by Christian Hubert. In *The Foucault reader*, edited by Paul Rabinow, 239–56. New York: Pantheon.

————. 1986. Of other spaces. Translated by Jay Miskowiec. *Diacritics* 16.1: 22–27.

Freud, Sigmund. 1971. "The 'uncanny.'" In *The standard edition of the complete psychological works of Sigmund Freud.* Vol. 17, 219–56. Translated by James Strachey. 1919. London: Hogarth Press.

————. 1975. *Three essays on the theory of sexuality.* 4th ed. Translated by James Strachey. New York: Basic Books.

Gasché, Rodolphe. 1994. *Inventions of difference: On Jacques Derrida.* Cambridge: Harvard University Press.

Gifford, Don. 1988. *"Ulysses" annotated.* Berkeley: University of California Press.

Godzich, Wlad. 1994. *The culture of literacy.* Cambridge: Harvard University.

Goldwater, Robert. 1986. *Primitivism in modern art.* Cambridge: Harvard University Press.

Gordon, Lyndall. 1977. *Eliot's early years.* New York: Oxford University Press.

Gray, Piers. 1982. *T. S. Eliot's intellectual and poetic development 1909–1922.* Brighton: Harvester Press.

Greenhalgh, Paul. 1988. *Ephemeral vistas: The 'expositions universelles,' great exhibitions and world's fairs, 1851–1939.* Manchester: Manchester University Press.

Gregory, Augusta. 1974. *Poets and dreamers: Studies and translations from the Irish.* 1903. New York: Oxford University Press.

Heath, Stephen. 1984. Ambiviolences: Notes for reading Joyce. Translated by Isabelle Mahieu. In *Post-structuralist Joyce: Essays from the French,* edited by Derek Attridge and Daniel Ferrer, 31–68. Cambridge: Cambridge University Press. First published in *Tel Quel* 50 (summer 1972): 22–43 and 51 (fall 1972): 64–76.

Heidegger, Martin. 1977. *The question concerning technology and other essays.* Translated by William Lovitt. New York: Harper and Row.

Herr, Cheryl. 1986. *Joyce's anatomy of culture.* Urbana: University of Illinois Press.

Irigaray, Luce. 1985. *This sex which is not one.* Translated by Catherine Porter. Ithaca, N. Y.: Cornell University Press.

Jameson, Fredric. 1979. *Fables of aggression: Wyndham Lewis, the modernist as fascist.* Berkeley: University of California Press.

———. 1981. *The political unconscious: Narrative as a socially symbolic act.* Ithaca, N.Y.: Cornell University Press.

Jones, Ernest. 1964. *Essays in applied psycho-analysis.* 2 vols. New York: International Universities Press.

Joyce, James. 1959. *Finnegans wake.* New York: Penguin.

———. 1968. *Giacomo Joyce.* London: Faber and Faber.

———. 1986. *Ulysses: The corrected text.* Edited by Hans Walter Gabler. London: Bodley Head.

———. 1989. *The critical writings.* Edited by Ellsworth Mason and Richard Ellmann. Ithaca, N.Y.: Cornell University Press.

———. 1992. *Dubliners.* New York: Penguin.

———. 1992. *A portrait of the artist as a young man.* Edited by Seamus Deane. New York: Penguin.

Kipling, Rudyard. 1898. The city of dreadful night. In *The writings in prose and verse,* vol. 4, 35–45. New York: Scribner's.

Krafft-Ebing, Richard von. 1947. *Psychopathia sexualis: A medico-forensic study.* Translated by F. J. Rebman. New York: Pioneer.

Kristeva, Julia. 1994. *Le temps sensible: Proust et l'expérience littéraire.* Paris: Gallimard.

Lacan, Jacques. 1976. Le sinthome. *Ornicar?* 7.

———. 1979. Joyce le symptôme. In *Joyce et Paris: Actes du cinquième symposium international James Joyce.* Paris: CNRS.

———. 1982. God and the jouissance of the woman. Translated by Jacqueline Rose. In *Feminine sexuality: Jacques Lacan and the ecole freudienne,* edited by Juliet Mitchell and Jacqueline Rose. New York: Norton.

Ledden, Patrick. 1994. Some comments on Vincent Cheng's "Empire and patriarchy in 'The Dead.'" *Joyce Studies Annual*: 202–7.

Leonard, Garry M. 1993. *Reading "Dubliners" again: A Lacanian perspective*. Syracuse: Syracuse University Press.

Lévinas, Emmanuel. 1989. *The Lévinas reader*. Edited by Sean Hand. Oxford: Blackwell.

Lévi-Strauss, Claude. 1955. *Tristes tropiques*. Paris: Plon.

———. 1962. *La pensée sauvage*. Paris: Plon.

Lévy-Bruhl, Lucien. 1899. *History of modern philosophy in France*. Translated by G. Coblence. London: Kegan Paul.

———. 1918. *Les fonctions mentales dans les sociétés inférieures*. 1910. Paris: Felix Alcan.

———. 1922. *La mentalité primitive*. Paris: Felix Alcan.

———. 1924. Primitive mentality and gambling. *Criterion* 2.6 (February): 188–200.

———. 1949. *Les carnets de Lévy-Bruhl*. Paris: Presses Universitaires de France.

Lewis, Wyndham. 1927. *Time and western man*. London: Chatto and Windus.

Littleton, C. Scott. 1985. Lucien Lévy-Bruhl and the concept of cognitive relativity. Introduction to *How natives think*, by Lucien Lévy-Bruhl, translated by Lilian A. Clare. Princeton: Princeton University Press.

Lloyd, David. 1993. *Anomalous states: Irish writing and the post-colonial moment*. Durham: Duke University Press.

Lukacher, Ned. 1986. *Primal scenes: Literature, history, psychoanalysis*. Ithaca, N.Y.: Cornell University Press.

Lyons, F.S.L. 1977. *Charles Stewart Parnell*. London: Collins.

Macaulay, Thomas Babington. 1898. *Works*. Vol. 9. London: Longmans Green.

MacCabe, Colin. 1979. *James Joyce and the revolution of the word*. New York: Barnes and Noble.

Mallarmé, Stéphane. 1945. *Oeuvres complètes*. Paris: Pléiade.

Manganaro, Marc. 1986. Dissociation in "Dead Land": The primitive mind in the early poetry of T. S. Eliot. *Journal of Modern Literature* 13: 97–110.

———. 1992. *Myth, rhetoric, and the voice of authority: A critique of Frazer, Eliot, Frye, and Campbell*. New Haven: Yale University Press.

Manganiello, Dominic. 1984. Anarch, heresiarch, egoarch. In *Joyce in Rome,* edited by Giorgio Melchiori, 98–115. Rome: Bulzoni Editore.

Margueritte, Paul. 1882. *Pierrot assassin de sa femme*. Paris: Paul Schmidt.

Martin, Graham, ed. 1970. *Eliot in perspective: A symposium*. New York: Humanities Press.

Maurer, Evan. 1984. Dada and surrealism. In *"Primitivism" in twentieth-century art: Affinity of the tribal and the modern,* edited by William Rubin, vol. 2, 535–94. New York: Museum of Modern Art.

McHugh, Roland. 1976. *The sigla of "Finnegans Wake."* Austin: University of Texas Press.

———. 1991. *Annotations to "Finnegans Wake."* Revised ed. Baltimore: Johns Hopkins University Press.

Meisel, Perry. 1987. *The myth of the modern: A study in British literature and criticism after 1850.* New Haven: Yale University Press.

Mercanton, Jacques. 1967. *Les heures de James Joyce.* Lausanne: L'Age d'Homme.

Mercier, Paul. 1984. *Histoire de l'anthropologie.* Paris: Presses Universitaires de France.

Mitchell, Timothy. 1988. *Colonising Egypt.* Cambridge: Cambridge University Press.

Monnerot, Jules. 1945. *La poésie moderne et le sacré.* Paris: Gallimard.

Moore, Thomas. 1929. *Poetical works.* Edited by A. D. Godley. Oxford: Oxford University Press.

Morel, E. D. 1906. *Red rubber: The story of the rubber slave trade flourishing on the Congo in the year of grace 1906.* London: Fisher Unwin.

O'Hegarty, P. S. 1952. *A history of Ireland under the Union.* London: Methuen.

Osteen, Mark. 1992. The money question at the back of everything: Cliches, counterfeits and forgeries in Joyce's "Eumaeus." *Modern Fiction Studies* 38.4: 821–43.

Parry, Benita. 1987. Problems in current theories of colonial discourse. *Oxford Literary Review* 9: 27–58.

Pound, Ezra. 1957. *Selected poems.* New York: New Directions.

Proust, Marcel. 1981. *Remembrance of things past.* Translated by C. K. Scott Moncrieff and Terence Kilmartin. 3 vols. New York: Random House.

———. 1982. *Correspondance.* Edited by Philip Kolb. Paris: Plon.

———. 1987. *Sésame et les lys.* Preface "Sur la lecture." Paris: Complexe.

———. 1988. *A la recherche du temps perdu.* Edited by Jean-Yves Tadié. 4 vols. Paris: Gallimard, Editions de la Pléiade.

Rabaté, Jean-Michel. 1984. Lapsus ex machina, translated by Elizabeth Guild. In *Post-structuralist Joyce: Essays from the French,* edited by Derek Attridge and Daniel Ferrer, 79–101. Cambridge: Cambridge University Press.

———. 1988. Paternity, thy name is Joy. In *The augmented Ninth: Proceedings of the Ninth International James Joyce Symposium,* edited by Bernard Benstock, 219–25. Syracuse: Syracuse University Press.

———. 1991. *James Joyce, authorized reader.* Baltimore: Johns Hopkins University Press.

Ragland-Sullivan, Ellie. 1990. Lacan's seminars on James Joyce: Writing as symptom and "singular solution." In *Psychoanalysis and . . . ,* edited by R. Feldstein and H. Sullivan. New York: Routledge. Quoted in Leonard, 7.

Rainey, Lawrence. 1996. Consuming investments: Joyce's "*Ulysses.*" *James Joyce Quarterly* 33.4: 531–68.

———. 1999. *Institutions of modernism: Literary elites and public culture.* New Haven: Yale University Press.

Ricks, Christopher. 1988. *T. S. Eliot and prejudice.* Berkeley: University of California Press.

Ruskin, John. 1920. *Sesame and lilies.* New York: Dutton.

————. 1991. *The stones of Venice.* In *Selected writings of John Ruskin,* edited by Kenneth Clark. London: Penguin.

Simmel, Georg. 1989. *Philosophie de la modernité.* Translated by Jean-Louis Vieillard-Baron. 2 vols. Paris: Payot.

Small, Helen. 1996. *The practice and representation of reading in England.* Cambridge University Press.

Smith, Grover, ed. 1963. *Josiah Royce's seminar, 1913–1914: As recorded in the notebooks of Harry T. Costello.* New Brunswick, N.J.: Rutgers University Press.

Smith, Vincent A. 1981. *The Oxford history of India.* 4th ed. Delhi: Oxford University Press.

Spurr, David. 1993. *The rhetoric of empire: Colonial discourse in journalism, travel writing, and imperial administration.* Durham: Duke University Press.

Stein, Gertrude. 1966. *The autobiography of Alice B. Toklas.* London: Penguin.

Sultan, Stanley. 1987. *Eliot, Joyce and company.* New York: Oxford University Press.

Tindall, William York. 1969. *A reader's guide to "Finnegans Wake."* New York: Farrar, Straus and Giroux.

van Boheemen-Saaf, Christine. 1988. Joyce, Derrida, and the discourse of "the other." In *The augmented Ninth: Proceedings of the Ninth International James Joyce Symposium,* edited by Bernard Benstock, 88–102. Syracuse: Syracuse University Press.

————. 1999. *Joyce, Derrida, Lacan, and the trauma of history.* Cambridge: Cambridge University Press.

Vanderham, Paul. 1998. *James Joyce and censorship: The trials of "Ulysses."* London: Macmillan.

Vickery, John B. 1973. *The literary impact of "The Golden Bough."* Princeton: Princeton University Press.

Vico, Giambattista. 1948. *The new science.* Translated by Thomas Bergin and Harold Fisch. Ithaca, N.Y.: Cornell University Press.

Wentinck, Charles. 1979. *Modern and primitive art.* Translated by Hilary Davies. Oxford: Phaidon.

Whitman, Walt. 1998. *Leaves of Grass.* Oxford: Oxford University Press.

Wilde, Oscar. 1986. *De profundis and other writings.* London: Penguin.

Žižek, Slavoj. 1993. *Tarrying with the negative: Kant, Hegel, and the critique of ideology.* Durham, N.C.: Duke University Press.

————. 1997. *The plague of fantasies.* London: Verso.

Index

David Spurr is professor of English at the University of Geneva, Switzerland. He is the author of *Conflicts in Consciousness: T. S. Eliot's Poetry and Criticism* (1984) and *The Rhetoric of Empire: Colonial Discourse in Journalism, Travel Writing, and Imperial Administration* (1993).

The Florida James Joyce Series
Edited by Zack Bowen

Joycean Temporalities: Debts, Promises, and Countersignatures, by Tony Thwaites (2001)

Joyce and the Victorians, by Tracey Teets Schwarze (2002)

Joyce's Ulysses *as National Epic: Epic Mimesis and the Political History of the Nation State,* by Andras Ungar (2002)

James Joyce's "Fraudstuff," by Kimberly J. Devlin (2002)

Rite of Passage in the Narratives of Dante and Joyce, by Jennifer Fraser (2002)

Joyce and the Scene of Modernity, by David Spurr (2002)